Tracing Your Great War Ancestors: The Somme

FAMILY HISTORY FROM PEN & SWORD BOOKS

Tracing Secret Service Ancestors

Tracing Your Air Force Ancestors

Tracing Your Ancestors

Tracing Your Ancestors from 1066 to 1837

Tracing Your Ancestors through Death Records

Tracing Your Ancestors through Family Photographs

Tracing Your Ancestors Using the Census

Tracing Your Ancestors' Childhood

Tracing Your Ancestors' Parish Records#

Tracing Your Aristocratic Ancestors

Tracing Your Army Ancestors - 2nd Edition

Tracing Your Birmingham Ancestors

Tracing Your Black Country Ancestors

Tracing Your British Indian Ancestors

Tracing Your Canal Ancestors

Tracing Your Channel Islands Ancestors

Tracing Your Coalmining Ancestors

Tracing Your Criminal Ancestors

Tracing Your East Anglian Ancestors

Tracing Your East End Ancestors

Tracing Your Edinburgh Ancestors

Tracing Your First World War Ancestors

Tracing Your Great War Ancestors: The Gallipoli Campaign

Tracing Your Great War Ancestors: The Somme

Tracing Your Great War Ancestors: Ypres

Tracing Your Huguenot Ancestors

Tracing Your Jewish Ancestors

Tracing Your Labour Movement Ancestors

Tracing Your Lancashire Ancestors

Tracing Your Leeds Ancestors

Tracing Your Legal Ancestors

Tracing Your Liverpool Ancestors

Tracing Your London Ancestors

Tracing Your Medical Ancestors

Tracing Your Merchant Navy Ancestors

Tracing Your Naval Ancestors

Tracing Your Northern Ancestors

Tracing Your Pauper Ancestors

Tracing Your Police Ancestors

Tracing Your Prisoner of War Ancestors: The First World War

Tracing Your Railway Ancestors

Tracing Your Royal Marine Ancestors

Tracing Your Rural Ancestors

Tracing Your Scottish Ancestors

Tracing Your Second World War Ancestors

Tracing Your Servant Ancestors

Tracing Your Service Women Ancestors

Tracing Your Shipbuilding Ancestors

Tracing Your Tank Ancestors

Tracing Your Textile Ancestors

Tracing Your Trade and Craftsmen Ancestors

Tracing Your Welsh Ancestors

Tracing Your West Country Ancestors

For more details see www.pen-and-sword.co.uk.

TRACING YOUR GREAT WAR ANCESTORS: THE SOMME

A Guide for Family Historians

SIMON FOWLER

Pen & Sword

FAMILY HISTORY

First published in Great Britain in 2015 by
Pen & Sword Family History
an imprint of
Pen & Sword Books Ltd
47 Church Street
Barnsley
South Yorkshire
S70 2AS

ISBN 978 1 47382 369 3

Typeset in 10pt Palatino by Mac Style Ltd, Bridlington, East Yorkshire
Printed and bound in the UK by CPI Group (UK) Ltd, Croydon, CRO 4YY

Pen & Sword Books Ltd incorporates the imprints of Pen & Sword
Archaeology, Atlas, Aviation, Battleground, Discovery, Family
History, History, Maritime, Military, Naval, Politics, Railways, Select,
Social History, Transport, True Crime, and Claymore Press, Frontline
Books, Leo Cooper, Praetorian Press, Remember When, Seaforth
Publishing and Wharncliffe.

For a complete list of Pen & Sword titles please contact
PEN & SWORD BOOKS LIMITED
47 Church Street, Barnsley, South Yorkshire, S70 2AS, England
E-mail: enquiries@pen-and-sword.co.uk
Website: www.pen-and-sword.co.uk

CONTENTS

LIST OF ABBREVIATIONS

Army paperwork is full of abbreviations that can be puzzling to the novice researcher.

ACI	Army Council Instruction
ADS	Advanced Dressing Station
AIF	Australian Imperial Force
ASC	Army Service Corps
BEF	British Expeditionary Corps
BRCS	British Red Cross Society
BWM	British War Medal
CEF	Canadian Expeditionary Force
CCS	Casualty Clearing Station
CLC	Chinese Labour Corps
CO	Commanding officer
Cpl	Corporal
Cpt	Captain
CQMS	Company Quartermaster Master Sergeant
CRA	Commanding Royal Artillery
CRE	Commanding Royal Engineers
CSM	Company Sergeant Major
FP	Field punishment
GCM	General Court Martial
GHQ	General Headquarters
GOC	General Officer Commanding
GSW	Gunshot Wound
HA	Heavy Artillery
HE	Heavy Explosive
HS	Home Service
HAC	Honourable Artillery Company
IOR	Indian Other Rank

KIA	Killed in Action
KR	King's Regulations
KRRC	King's Royal Rifle Corps
L/Cpl	Lance Corporal
LofC	Lines of communication
L/Sgt	Lance Sergeant
Lt	Lieutenant
Lt Col	Lieutenant Colonel
MGC	Machine Gun Corps
MiD	Mentioned in Despatches
NCO	Non-commissioned Officer
OC	Officer commanding
OR	Other Rank
PBI	Poor Bloody Infantry
POW	Prisoner of War
Pte	Private
PU	Permanently unfit (found in service records)
QAIMNS	Queen Alexandra's Imperial Military Nursing Service
QARNNC	Queen Alexandra's Royal Naval Nursing Corps
RA	Royal Artillery
RAF	Royal Air Force
RAMC	Royal Army Medical Corps
RE	Royal Engineers
RFC	Royal Flying Corps
RFA	Royal Field Artillery
RGA	Royal Garrison Artillery
RHA	Royal Horse Artillery
RNAS	Royal Naval Air Service
RND	Royal Naval Division
SAA	Small Arms Ammunition
Sgt	Sergeant
TF	Territorial Force
VAD	Voluntary Aid Detachment
WAAC	Women's Army Auxiliary Corps
WO	War Office

The Long Long Trail provides a comprehensive list of abbreviations at www.1914-1918.net/abbrev.htm

INTRODUCTION

This is a book about the Western Front in France and how to research the men who served there and the actions that took place along the sixty or so miles of trenches between the Belgian border near Armentières and the River Somme, where French troops took over responsibility for the Western Front. It is the third in a series: the other volumes cover

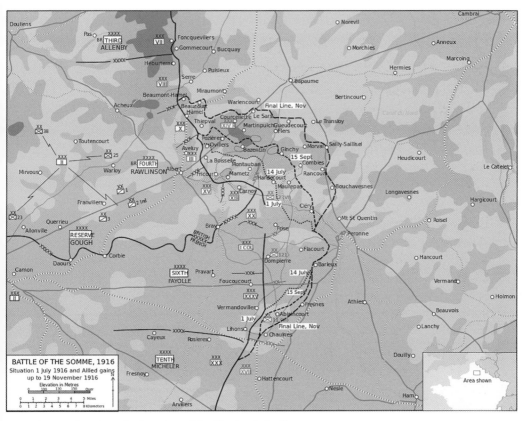

A map showing the location of the Battle of the Somme.

Going over the top on 1 July 1916. It is almost certain this photograph is actually of a training exercise.

Gallipoli and Ypres (that is Flanders, or Belgium). There is of course considerable overlap between the books, particularly between those covering Ypres and the Somme. Most British Army units spent time in both Flanders and France, generally unaware in which country they were stationed.

As with the companion volumes this book is designed for the person starting out researching individuals or units. If you are looking for arcane discussions on the design of medal cards or the value of the Silver War Badge then you have come to the wrong place (but see the bibliography).

The British Army used the words 'casualty' and 'casualties' to mean soldiers who became ineffective for one reason or another; it did not only mean being killed (which is how we tend to use the words now), but also men who were wounded, missing in action or who were taken prisoner of war.

In describing the records I have used individuals and units that fought in France as examples of what can be discovered. I have tried to include a wide variety of individuals: conscripts, volunteers and the pre-war regulars, whose discipline and marksmanship slowed the German advance towards Paris in the autumn of 1914 and who paid grievously for their heroism.

The main difference between Ypres and the Somme lies in the topography, although this had surprisingly little effect on the fighting itself, partly, perhaps, because the Germans occupied the high ground where possible at both places, which meant a long dangerous slog uphill for the advancing troops. The experiences in the trenches around Ypres can simply be described in one word: mud. The landscape of France is much more varied, although of course there was plenty of mud here as well. The Marne, where the British Army fought valiantly in September 1914, comprises attractive heavily wooded hills and deep valleys. The poet John Masefield described the high-lying chalk landscape of the Somme as being 'something like the downland of Berkshire and Buckinghamshire, though generally barer of trees, and less bold in its valleys.' And between the Somme and the Belgian frontier, where the Battle of Loos was fought in the autumn of 1915, lay a plain of coalmines and grim industrial villages.

The battlefield as it appeared in October 1916 shortly after the Schwaben Redoubt was taken by the British. It lay between Thiepval Memorial and the Ulster Tower memorial.

The site of the village of Guillemont was taken by British forces on 3 September 1916. Nothing remained of the village but a few ruins.

The region will always be remembered for the Battle of the Somme, which began on 1 July 1916. This book does not attempt to provide a history of actions or battles. Fortunately there are many excellent books available which describe what went on in greater or lesser detail; key titles are listed in the bibliography.

No study of an individual or unit is complete unless you go to see where they fought. Geoff Dyer wrote of his visits to the battlefields: '…I know that some part of me will always be calmed by the memory of this place, by the vast capacity for forgiveness revealed by these cemeteries, by this landscape.' After nearly a century there are few physical reminders of the fighting, except the cemeteries and the memorials, which were largely constructed in the 1920s, but there are many excellent museums and other attractions. I have attempted to describe the most important and interesting of these.

Simon Fowler
September 2015

Websites

Certain key websites are constantly referred to throughout the book. To prevent needless repetition they are listed below together with their web addresses:

Ancestry	www.ancestry.co.uk
Commonwealth War Graves Commission	www.cwgc.org
Findmypast	www.findmypast.co.uk
Forces War Records	www.forces-war-records.co.uk
Long Long Trail	www.1914-1918.net
The Genealogist	www.thegenealogist.co.uk
The National Archives	www.nationalarchives.gov.uk
Naval & Military Archives	www.nmarchive.com

Chapter 1

GETTING STARTED

This chapter offers basic guidance for researching soldiers or the units they served in.

Online Resources

There are several major data providers with significant First World War content online that are likely to be of use to family historians: Ancestry, Findmypast, and The National Archives. Which one you choose depends on what you are looking for, which may of course include records that do not necessarily relate to the First World War.

The home page for Ancestry's First World War collections. Ancestry has one of the largest collections of material for the Great War.

Ancestry (www.ancestry.co.uk) is undoubtedly the best place to start. It is a subscription site: you pay for a year's unlimited access to the data. If you are not already a subscriber it is worth trying the free fourteen-day trial. Alternatively, access is free at many local libraries. However, it is of little use if your interest is not primarily genealogical. With some exceptions much the same material is available on Findmypast (www.findmypast.co.uk). It is also a subscription site with a fourteen-day free membership deal, and both sites give occasional free access to the First World War information. If you are only interested in Findmypast's First World War material then you might want to subscribe through the Lives of the First World War website (www.livesofthefirstworldwar.org), where membership is half the price it would be through the main website.

Lives of the First World War

Lives of the First World War is an ambitious joint project by the Imperial War Museum and Findmypast. The intention is for people to put up memories and other details of family members who fought during the First World War. In order to do this you need to sign up, which is free. Registration has the added benefit of enabling very basic access to some key First World War records, notably the Medal Index Cards (although the dataset is by no means complete). You can also subscribe to get access to all of the First World War records provided by Findmypast and additional functionality on the website. The subscription is currently £50 per year.

Unfortunately, the project has not proven to be a great success. At the time of writing there were fewer than 70,000 subscribers, who had posted details of some 125,000 men; fewer than two per cent of the men who served in the British Army between 1914 and 1919. Matters are not helped by the rather convoluted way you have to submit information, which rather defeated me when I tried to add data and a photograph of my great-uncles. However, you may consider it worth joining and adding material about your First World War ancestors.

www.livesofthefirstworldwar.org

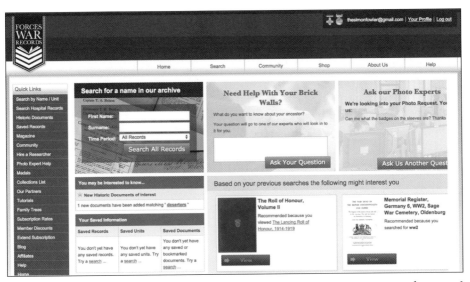

Forces War Records is one of the smaller providers of information about men who served in the First World War. Of particular interest are the Hospital Records.

Findmypast also operates Genes Reunited, but the records are much the same as on the main website.

The National Archives (TNA) provides online access to service records for men who served in the Royal Navy and the Royal Air Force and the women who joined the services during the war. You can also download war diaries, cabinet papers (if you are interested in the strategic and diplomatic aspects of the War), and air combat reports. Some material is free, such as the Cabinet papers, but in general you pay to download specific documents, which come as PDFs. At time of writing the cost was £3.30 per document. A document might be just a single-page service record, or hundreds of pages of a war diary. A word of warning: war diaries tend to come in huge files, which can take hours to download if you do not have superfast broadband. An increasing proportion of the material from TNA is also available through Findmypast.

If your interest is solely in the First World War then you might consider the Naval and Military Archive (www.nmarchive.com), from Naval and Military Press, or Forces War Records (www.forces-war-records.co.uk). In addition there is *The Genealogist* (www.thegenealogist.co.uk), which has incomplete sets of the War Office Weekly Casualty Lists and Military

Medal cards, together with Medal Index Cards and various other minor datasets. However, in all cases there is some overlap with data on Ancestry and Findmypast.

Resources in Archives

Not everything is online by any means. If you decide to do an in-depth study of an individual, or research a particular unit or action, you are likely to need to use original papers, letters and files that will be found in an archive. If you want to know more about what archives are and how to use them there is a series of Quick Animated Guides at www.nationalarchives.gov.uk/records/quick-animated-guides.htm.

The Document Reading Room of The National Archives, where you can consult original records from medieval times to the present. (*Author*)

There are three major types of archive, with some overlap between their holdings. The most important is The National Archives in Kew, which has almost all the surviving service and operational records for the three services (Army, Navy and Air Force), plus much else besides. In this book assume that the records described are held by The National Archives (TNA) unless indicated otherwise. There is an excellent website – www.nationalarchives.gov.uk – which will help you find the records you are looking for and prepare for a visit. In particular, detailed Research Guides explain the records very simply. Find them at www.national archives.gov.uk/records.

The records themselves are described via the Discovery catalogue. The catalogue describes all eleven million documents available for researchers at Kew. Descriptions are often pretty general, but should be good enough for you to be able to work out which pieces are likely to be useful. An increasing number of documents are available indexed by individual, such as the service men and women (as well as a few civilians) who appear in the Medal Index Cards. Of course, just because there is no mention of an individual in Discovery does not mean there is nothing about them at Kew.

Regimental and service museums and archives have records relating to specific services or regiments. The big service museums are the Imperial War Museum (for all services), the National Army Museum and the RAF Museum. Addresses are given below. In addition there is the Royal Naval Museum in Portsmouth, although it has little about the Western Front.

The National Army Museum also has some papers from the Irish regiments disbanded in 1922 (that is the Royal Dublin and Royal Munster Fusiliers, Connaught Rangers, Royal Leinster and Royal Irish regiments and the South Irish Horse), the Indian Army (whose records are shared with the British Library), Middlesex Regiment and the East Kent Regiment (The Buffs). However, the museum is closed for rebuilding until late 2016 and access to their archives is currently limited as a result.

Most regiments also have their own regimental museum and archive, although their archives are increasingly to be found at the appropriate county record office. These archives may include collections of regimental orders, personal papers and photographs, unit war diaries (which may duplicate those at Kew), regimental magazines, registers and other records which TNA, for one reason or another, did not want. Each of these archives has very different collections, so you may strike lucky or leave almost empty-handed. Most museums and archives welcome visitors, but you usually have to make an appointment. The Army Museums Ogilby Trust maintains a very good website (www.armymuseums.org.uk), which links to museum websites and provides details about individual regimental museums.

Service and regimental museums *do not hold* any service records: these are either at TNA or, for men who left after the end of 1920, with the Ministry of Defence.

County archives (or record offices) may have material, particularly relating to the impact of the war on local communities. A few have archives deposited by the local regiment: the Durham County Record Office, for example, has records of the Durham Light Infantry. There may also be records of territorial regiments, which provided many of the soldiers who served in France in 1915 and 1916, rolls of honour and files about war memorials.

There are also many more specialist repositories ranging from the British Library, which is comparable to The National Archives in size and importance, to company and hospital archives. With the exception of the British Library, which has records of the Indian Army, these are not likely to hold much direct information about the First World War.

Contact details for all British archives can be found on the Discovery catalogue on the TNA website, although you will need to scroll down to find the right search box. For regimental museums, however, it may be easier to go via www.armymuseums.org.uk.

As well as indexes to material at TNA, Discovery also contains details of many records at local record offices. You need to be aware of this when using the catalogue, because unless you are careful it will produce results for material at both Kew and local archives. However, by no means everything at local archives is described here. For example, there are 223 entries relating to the Somme, ranging from postcards of villages in the area at the Derbyshire Record Office, to the papers of the 'Worksop Poet' Sgt John William Streets, who was killed on 1 July 1916, at the Nottinghamshire Archives (Neither of these is on Discovery). Examples of Streets' poems, as well as a brief biography, can be found at www.greatwar.co.uk/people/john-william-streets.htm.

The holdings of archives in Wales are described at www.archives networkwales.info. In Scotland the Scottish Archive Network provides something similar at www.scan.org.uk.

Using online catalogues can be tricky, particularly those provided by local record offices, so if there is a help page it is a good idea to read it before you start. In general the more information you type in, the more it will confuse the search engine, so try to keep it simple.

Genealogical Records

It is easy to overlook the basic genealogical sources of birth, marriage and death records, census returns and wills in researching soldiers, but they are also worth checking out. And of course many researchers first become aware of having military ancestors from an entry in the census or on a marriage certificate.

Most of these records are now available online, or are likely to become so in the foreseeable future.

The Census

Census records are an important source for family history, revealing unique information about ancestors. In particular, because it was taken so close to the outbreak of the First World War, the 1911 census is a key source. The English and Welsh census is available through Findmypast and Ancestry. You should be able to find details of an individual's civilian career and those who were living with him. John William Streets was a coal miner (hewer) in 1911, living with his parents and eleven brothers and sisters. VC winner Theodore Veale also lived at home with his parents and was following his father into the building trade.

The Scottish 1911 census is at ScotlandsPeople (www.scotlandspeople. gov.uk) and the Irish census is at www.census.nationalarchives.ie. The information in all three censuses is almost identical and they are fully indexed so it is pretty easy to find an ancestor.

The 1911 census is unique for another reason. For the first time servicemen and their families serving overseas in both the Navy and the Army were recorded. Soldiers' names, age, rank and place of birth were recorded. Of particular interest are the returns for army wives and children. This is the first census for which such records exist. To access the military returns, in the appropriate box on the search screen tick 'Overseas military'.

The entry for John William Streets in the 1911 Census. He is recorded as being a 25-year old coal hewer living at home with his parents and younger brothers and sisters. (*Ancestry/The National Archives*)

Birth, Marriage and Death Certificates

National registration began in England and Wales on 1 July 1837 (Scotland – 1855, Ireland – 1864). The system has remained largely unchanged since then. You can order certificates for men who were killed in action or died of wounds during the First World War. However, there is little point as they won't tell you anything you don't know already.

English and Welsh certificates can be ordered online at www.gro. gov.uk/gro/content/certificates/default.asp, or by phone (0300 123 1837). Scottish ones are all online through ScotlandsPeople. Indexes to Irish births, marriages and deaths for the period (both North and South) are available through FamilySearch (www.familysearch.org), but you have to order the certificates from the General Register Office for Ireland (www.groireland.ie). This can be done online at www.hse.ie/eng/ services/list/1/bdm/Certificate.

Also of interest are Chaplains' Returns and Army Register Books recording births, baptisms, marriages, deaths and burials of soldiers and their families at home and abroad. Indexes are at www.findmypast.com and TNA.

The National Archives also holds a small number of regimental registers of births, baptisms, marriages and burials in series WO 156, which are online at Deceased Online (www.deceasedonline.co.uk).

Wills

It was naturally important for soldiers to make wills before going into action. Indeed the army pay book, which was issued to all soldiers, included a simple will form which could be completed. Generally any possessions were left to the individual's wife or next of kin.

There may well be papers about wills and the disposal of personal effects in the files of individual officers and soldiers. If an individual made a will that was proved in the Principal Probate Registry, then details were published in the National Probate Calendars. The Calendars are online at Ancestry. Wills themselves cost £10 (at time of writing) and can be ordered by post from the Leeds District Probate Registry, York House, 31 York Place, Leeds, LS1 2BA.

In addition the Probate Registry has released some 200,000 wills that were made by soldiers in the field. There is an index at www.gov.uk/probate-search. Again you can order copies online for £10 each.

The National Records of Scotland has a collection of 30,000 wills for Scottish soldiers. There is an online index, although you can only see digital images of the originals in the reading rooms. For more details see www.nas.gov.uk/guides/searchSoldiersWills.asp. The Irish National Archives has some 9,000 wills available at http://soldierswills.national archives.ie/search/sw/home.jsp.

Useful Addresses

British Library, 96 Euston Road, London NW1 2DB; www.bl.uk

Imperial War Museum, Lambeth Road, London SE1 6HZ; www.iwm. org.uk

The National Archives, Ruskin Avenue, Kew, Richmond TW9 4DU; www.nationalarchives.gov.uk

National Army Museum, Royal Hospital Road, London SW3 4HT; www.national-army-museum.org.uk. The museum is closed until late 2016 for rebuilding so there is only limited access to their archival collections.

RAF Museum, Graeme Park Way, London NW9 5LL; www.rafmuseum. org.uk

Royal Naval Museum, HM Naval Base, Portsmouth PO1 3NH; www.royalnavalmuseum.org/research.htm

Army Museums Ogilby Trust; www.armymuseums.org.uk

Over the Top

Lt Edward Liveing, of 1/12th London Regiment, was among the first wave of troops who went over the top near Gommecourt on 1 July 1916.

We could not see properly over the top of the trench, but smoke was going over. The attack was about to begin – it was beginning. I passed word round the corner of the traverse, asking whether they could see if the second wave was starting. It was just past 7.30am. The third wave, of which my platoon formed a part, was due to start at 7.30 plus 45 seconds – at the same time as the second wave in my part of the line. The corporal got up, so I realized that the second wave was assembling on the top to go over. The ladders had been smashed or used as stretchers long ago. Scrambling out of a battered part of the trench, I arrived on top, looked down my line of men, swung my rifle forward as a signal, and started off at the prearranged walk.

A continuous hissing noise all around one, like a railway engine letting off steam, signified that the German machine-gunners had become aware of our advance. I nearly trod on a motionless form. It lay in a natural position, but the ashen face and fixed, fearful eyes told me that the man had just fallen. I did not recognize him then. I remember him now. He was one of my own platoon.

To go back for a minute. The scene that met my eyes as I stood on the parapet of our trench for that one second is almost indescribable. Just in front the ground was pitted by innumerable shell-holes. More holes opened

---

suddenly every now and then. Here and there a few bodies lay about. Farther away, before our front line and in No Man's Land, lay more. In the smoke one could distinguish the second line advancing. One man after another fell down in a seemingly natural manner, and the wave melted away. In the background, where ran the remains of the German lines and wire, there was a mass of smoke, the red of the shrapnel bursting amid it. Amongst it, I saw Captain H__ and his men attempting to enter the German front line. The Boches had met them on the parapet with bombs. The whole scene reminded me of battle pictures, at which in earlier years I had gazed with much amazement. Only this scene, though it did not seem more real, was infinitely more terrible. Everything stood still for a second, as a panorama painted with three colours: the white of the smoke, the red of the shrapnel and blood, the green of the grass.

If I had felt nervous before, I did not feel so now, or at any rate not in anything like the same degree. As I advanced, I felt as if I was in a dream, but I had all my wits about me. We had been told to walk. Our boys, however, rushed forward with splendid impetuosity to help their comrades and smash the German resistance in the front line. What happened to our materials for blocking the German communication trench, when we got to our objective, I should not like to think. I kept up a fast walking pace and tried to keep the line together. This was impossible. When we had jumped clear of the remains of our front line trench, my platoon slowly disappeared through the line stretching out. For a long time, however, Sergeant S__l, Lance-corporal M__, Rifleman D__, whom I remember being just in front of me, raising his hand in the air and cheering, and myself kept together. Eventually Lance-corporal M__ was the only one of my platoon left near me, and I shouted out to him, 'Let's try and keep together'. It was not long, however, before we also parted company. One thing I remember very well about this time, and that was that a hare jumped up and rushed towards and past me through the dry, yellowish grass, its eyes bulging with fear.

We were dropping into a slight valley. The shell-holes were less few, but bodies lay all over the ground, and a terrible groaning arose from all sides. At one time we seemed to be advancing in little groups. I was at the head of one for a moment or two, only to realize shortly afterwards that I was alone...

Suddenly I cursed. I had been scalded in the left hip. A shell, I thought, had blown up in a water-logged crump-hole and sprayed me with boiling water. Letting go of my rifle, I dropped forward full length on the ground. My hip began to smart unpleasantly, and I felt a curious warmth stealing down my left leg. I thought it was the boiling water that had scalded me. Certainly my breeches looked as if they were saturated with water. I did not know that they were saturated with blood.

So I lay, waiting with the thought that I might recover my strength (I could barely move) and try to crawl back. There was the greater possibility of death, but there was also the possibility of life. I looked around to see what was happening. In front lay some wounded; on either side of them stakes and shreds of barbed wire twisted into weird contortions by the explosions of our trench-mortar bombs. Beyond this nothing but smoke, interspersed with the red of bursting bombs and shrapnel.

From out this ghastly chaos crawled a familiar figure. It was that of Sergeant K__, bleeding from a wound in the chest. He came crawling towards me.

'Hallo, K__,' I shouted.

'Are you hit, sir?' he asked.

'Yes, old chap, I am,' I replied.

Taken from Edward D. Liveing, *Attack! A Subaltern's Impressions of July 1, 1916* (New York, 1918)

Chapter 2

RESEARCHING SOLDIERS

In this chapter we look at the basic records you can use to get a general picture of your ancestors' service.

Nearly six million men (and fifty thousand women) served in the British Army during the First World War, many of whom saw service in on the Somme or elsewhere in France. Although some records are missing, you should be able to find something about each of them, provided they served overseas. However, exactly what you will find cannot be predicted with any certainty. What survives varies greatly, which is one of the great charms of researching the First World War, although it can be frustrating if you find there is very little about your man.

Before you start you need to be reasonably confident of the soldier's full name, the regiment or other unit he served with, and – ideally – his service number (that is, if he was an ordinary soldier or non-commissioned officer). Otherwise it is can be very easy to start researching the wrong person.

It is important to remember all the possible variations of a man's name. After many years using the records I have come to the conclusion that if Army clerks *can* get soldiers' names wrong then they *will*. To take a simple example, although he was known to his family and friends as William, the Worksop Poet's full name was John William Streets, and this is how he is recorded in Army records. And my Great Uncle Stanley was properly Henry Philip Stanley Crozier, but he is in the records as Henry P.S., or just H.P.

If you have a soldier's medals, the information should be stamped on the rim or back. Or details may appear on family papers such as letters and diaries, or even written on the back of photographs. Family stories can also help, although often they are only general statements, such as, 'he was at the First Day on the Somme', or 'he was in the trenches when he was buried by an explosion,' which are obviously which not very useful. Even so they may offer a clue.

Each man's records are different and you never know what you are going to find. In general, however, there is likely to be more information on men who enlisted early in the war, saw frontline service, or who were killed in action.

Fowler's Rules for Military Genealogy

Here are five basic rules that might help you in your own research.

- The records for each serviceman and woman are different. There is no discernible rhyme or reason for what survives and what doesn't.
- The closer your ancestor was to the fighting, the more likely there are to be records about him and his experiences.
- There are more records about the fallen than those who survived, so in general it is easier to trace men who were killed in action and, to a lesser extent, those who died of wounds.
- It is easier to research men who volunteered – that is who had joined up by March 1916 – than those who were conscripted.
- Finally, there are always exceptions…

Medal Index Cards

Every serviceman and woman (as well as a few civilians) who saw service overseas was entitled to two campaign medals, the British War Medal and the Victory Medal. In addition men who had seen service in France and Flanders between 5 August and midnight on 22/23 November 1914 were awarded the 1914 Star (sometimes erroneously called the Mons Star), and men who served overseas between 5 August 1914 and 31 December 1915 were entitled to the 1914/15 Star. Occasionally you may find a reference to the Territorial Force War Medal, which was awarded to men who were members of the Territorial Forces at the beginning of the war and later who saw service overseas, but were not eligible for the 1914 or 1914/15 stars. My Great Uncle Stanley Crozier was one such recipient – his territorial unit served in India throughout the war, although Stanley managed to get a posting to 'France and Flanders', possibly in late 1916 or early 1917.

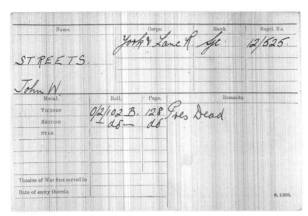

The Medal Index Card for Sgt John William Streets indicates that he was entitled to the British War and Allied Victory medals. The most interesting entry is a note indicating that he was presumed dead. (*Ancestry/ The National Archives*)

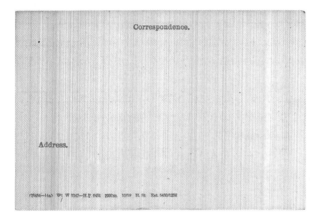

Each medal was stamped with the man's name and rank and number current at the time of his discharge. Details of individual recipients are to be found in the Medal Rolls and on Medal Index Cards. If you can't find a man's name then you can assume that for one reason or another he did not leave the British Isles.

There are several designs of Medal Index Card, but regardless of which design you come across it should tell you: the rank he held at the end of his service; regimental numbers (other ranks only); the units he served in; the medals to which he was entitled together with the page on the medal roll where details are to be found; the date he went overseas (if this was before the end of 1915); and the theatre of war in which he served. The Western Front was shown as 'F&F' for 'France and Flanders', or the number 1 or 1A. If no theatre is shown then he went to France.

In addition there may be information such as: the date of discharge or when he was killed in action (KIA); died of wounds (DofW); or occasionally, as with William Streets, presumed missing; the gallantry medals a man was awarded, whether he was entitled to wear the oak leaf emblem on the Victory Medal for being Mentioned in Despatches, usually abbreviated to EMB; a note he was entitled to wear a clasp (actually a silver rose) on his 1914 Star, which indicates that he had served within the sound of enemy guns, usually indicated by the word 'clasp'; whether he was discharged to the Z Reserve in 1919 (that is, he could be recalled in the event of resumption of hostilities with Germany).

There may also be heavily abbreviated notes about correspondence with the medal holder or his family generally, about which medals the individual was entitled to. On Great Uncle Stanley's card there is a note that a duplicate British War Medal had erroneously been sent to his family. Any correspondence has long since been destroyed.

The Cards are available online at both Ancestry (which calls them 'British Army WWI Medal Rolls Index Cards'), *The Genealogist* and via the TNA website. Ancestry offers by far the better reproduction, in colour, and provides both sides of each card, which occasionally includes the address to which the medals were sent and perhaps other notes. For Lt Edward G.D. Liveing, for example, there are notes that he had applied for the 1914–15 Star in 1920.

In addition Findmypast has an index with brief details, which links to images on the TNA website. The same index is available free of charge, if you register, on the Lives of the First World War website https://livesof thefirstworldwar.org/dashboard

Further reading

Peter Dicker, *British Campaign Medals of the First World War* (Shire, 2011)
Howard Williamson, *Great War Medal Collectors Companion* (3 vols) (Anne Williamson, 2012–2014)

Medal Rolls

The medal rolls, to which the cards refer, are at TNA, with copies online with both Ancestry (referred to as the 'WWI Service Medal and Award

Rolls, 1914–1920') and the Naval and Military Archive ('Campaign Medal Rolls'). In general, the only additional information you are likely to discover is the infantry battalion he was serving in at the time of his death or discharge. However, this will help you find the appropriate battalion war diary. Occasionally there is other information, such as reason for discharge or, less frequently, whether a man forfeited his medals because he was a deserter. The roll for the Connaught Rangers notes that Pte John Mayberry was discharged on 12 June 1916, because he was physically unfit for further service. Unfortunately it is rare to find any additional information if your man did not serve in the infantry.

Service Records: Other Ranks and Non-Commissioned Officers

Fewer than one in three service or personnel records for individual men survive. The remainder were destroyed during the Blitz. Even so they are worth searching out, because they provide a lot of additional information.

Individual files contain a wide range of paperwork, which can be informative if at times a little bewildering, but with a little practice and patience you should be able to decipher the forms and build up an intimate portrait of the individual. They certainly repay close study.

No two files are the same. Some are very detailed with a variety of forms, letters and other paperwork. But in other cases you may only find a man's attestation form or perhaps a medical record.

Of particular importance is the attestation form, completed by the individual on enlistment. This will indicate when and where a man enlisted and was discharged, as well as giving other personal details such as civilian occupation, home address and date of birth. It usually appears at the beginning of a service record.

If a man was a pre-war regular soldier, a part-time member of the Territorial Army, or had been recalled to the colours, then the file may include his pre-war attestation form (and details of his pre-war service), which might go back to the Boer War or even earlier.

The other form to look out for is Form B103/1 'Casualty Form – Active Service'. Despite the name it includes far more than wounds and stays in hospital. John William Streets appears to have been entirely healthy during his Army service, while Teddy Veale had any number of minor complaints and ailments before he gained his Victoria Cross and none

STATEMENT of the SERVICES of No. 5 2 5. Name John William								
Corps in which served	Regt. or Depôt	Promotions, Reductions, Casualties, &c.	Army Rank	Dates	Service not allowed to reckon for fixing the rate of Pension		Service in Reserve not allowed to reckon towards G. C. Pay	Signature of Officer certifying correctness of Entries
					years	days	years	days
		Service towards limited engagement reckons from		15·9·1914				
		Joined at Sheffield on		15·9·1914				
YORK & LANCASTER REGT.								
12th		attested	Pte.	15·9·1914				
12th				25·11·1914				
12th		promoted						
12		appointed	Lce Sgt.	5·5·1916				
12		appointed	a/Sergt	17·5·1916				
12		promoted	Sergt	6·6·1916				

Casualty form found in the service record for Sgt John William Streets. It gives the dates when he was promoted. Unusually there are no entries relating to wounds or illnesses, which suggests that Streets was unusually healthy. (*Ancestry/The National Archives*)

thereafter, (which suggests that the complaints may really have been of a psychological nature). Private Joseph John Streets of the 2/14th London Regiment (London Scottish) received a gunshot wound in his thigh on 1 July 1916, but recovered to be sent to Salonika, where he contracted trench fever. However, like Teddy Veale he survived the war.

The file may also tell you about: promotions through the ranks (and demotions if appropriate); the units he served in; when he went overseas and often when he was discharged; periods of leave; and notes of disciplinary offences (generally for drunkenness, petty theft or ignoring an officer's order). You may also find the date and reason for death or discharge. If he is discharged then there should be a reference to the appropriate sub-paragraph of King's Regulation 392 (see pp. 49–51 for a list of reasons).

If a man died during his Army service there may be correspondence and forms about his will and personal effects, as well as perhaps letters from the next of kin seeking more information about the circumstances of the loss of their man. For John William Streets his family were sent: 'letters,

2 diaries, postcards, 2 books of poems, sermon, photos, cover.' Some of these items are now with Nottinghamshire Archives.

What the records will not do is to tell you very much about any fighting a soldier was engaged in or any gallantry medals awarded. Nor will it give you any real idea of his life in the Army. However you can use the war diaries (see Chapter Six) to obtain this information.

Service records are online at both Ancestry and Findmypast. They are reasonably easy to use, although you might become frustrated by the extraneous names of next of kin and children that both companies have added to their indexes to make the collections seem more complete than they actually are.

Records for soldiers and non-commissioned officers of the Household Cavalry (which include the Life Guards, Royal Horse Guards and Household Battalion) are available through The National Archives Online Collections.

The five guards regiments (Coldstream, Grenadiers, Irish, Scottish and Welsh guards) still keep their own service records. You will need to contact the appropriate regimental headquarters at Wellington Barracks, Birdcage Walk, London SW1E 6HQ. When writing you must specify the regiment in the address. However, some guardsmen are to be found in the general collection of army service records.

If your man continued to serve in the Army after the end of 1920 his service record is still with the Ministry of Defence. Full details are available at www.veterans-uk.info.

Officers' Service Records

Surviving service records (about 85 per cent of the total) are at The National Archives in two series, WO 339 and WO 374. In practice there seems to be little difference between the two series. There is just one file for each officer. They are not online, but it is fairly easy to find individual references through TNA's Discovery Catalogue. In addition files for a few notable individuals, including Field Marshal Lord Haig and the poet Wilfred Owen, are in series WO 138. Most records of Guards officers are still with the appropriate regimental archives.

At some stage the records were weeded and much material was destroyed. Records for men who survived are generally less full than for

Army Service Numbers (regimental numbers)

Each ordinary soldier was given a regimental number when he enlisted. It was one of the ways he was identified in documents and on his identity tag if he was killed in action. Even today it helps considerably if you know your ancestors' service numbers, particularly if you are researching men with common names.

Until 1920 each regiment maintained its own system of numbering. When a man changed regiment, he was given a new service number.

As a very rough guide, the lower his number, the earlier a man enlisted. John William Streets' regimental number was 525, which indicates that he was probably the 525th man to enlist in the 'Sheffield Pals', the Sheffield City Battalion (formally 12th (Service) Battalion, York and Lancaster Regiment) when recruitment began on 10 September 1914.

A few regimental archives have recruitment registers listing recruits in regimental number order.

In addition regiments introduced a number of different prefixes to help differentiate the flood of new recruits in 1914 and later. The most common letter was G for General Service (that is for the duration of the war), followed by T for temporary or Territorial Army. A list of prefixes can be found at www.1914-1918.net/prefixes.html.

Officers were not given service numbers during the First World War.

those who died in action. Even so there may be correspondence concerning money, length of service and pensions, rather than about an individual's war service. If an officer came through the ranks then there should be his original enlistment document and recommendation from his commanding officer. If a man died during his service there are likely to be papers relating to the administration of his will and dispersal of his effects, as well as correspondence with the next-of-kin who were often trying to find out the circumstances of their son, brother or husband's death.

Officers are also listed in the Army Lists. This is an easy way to confirm whether an ancestor was an officer, because the Lists include everyone who was commissioned. They will reveal which regiment or unit he was

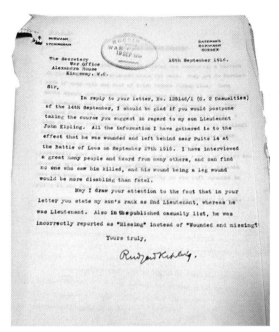

A letter from Rudyard Kipling found in the service record of his son Lt John Kipling, who was killed in action during the Battle of Loos in September 1915. It is not uncommon to find such letters in the personnel files of officers who made the ultimate sacrifice. (*The National Archives WO 339/53917*)

with, his rank and when he was promoted. The National Archives has a complete set on the shelves in the Open Reading Room, and copies can be found at the Imperial War Museum, National Army Museum and some regimental museums. There are sets online available through the Internet Archive at www.archive.org and volumes for 1914, 1915 and 1916 on *The Genealogist*. Neither set is particularly easy to use.

The *London Gazette* is the government's official newspaper. It includes announcements of the appointment of officers and any subsequent promotions, together with when and how they were discharged. The surnames and initials of individual officers are given, together with their regiment and the date the promotion (even if temporary) took place. Inevitably publication may be months after the event took place, but will always give the date the promotion was granted. A brief reason for the officer's resignation is often given. The *London Gazette* has been digitised and is online at www.thegazette.co.uk. Unfortunately the website is poorly designed and the indexing is unreliable, so you might want to run a site-specific search using Google (e.g. search for 'William Henry Johnston' site:thegazette.co.uk)

The Royal Naval Division

The Royal Naval Division (RND) was initially set up to use reservists for whom there were no places on board ships, although most members were recruits who preferred to enlist in the Navy than the Army. They served at Gallipoli and were transferred to the Army as 63rd (Royal Naval) Division in 1916, where they fought during the tail end of the Battle of the Somme and the subsequent battle of Ancrem before being transferred to Flanders. Individual brigades were named after naval heroes. The RND retained many naval traditions, to the intense annoyance of the Army high command, even while on land. They flew the White Ensign, used bells to signal time, used naval language (including 'going ashore' and 'coming on board' for leaving and arriving in the trenches), preferred naval ranks to army equivalents and sat during the toast to the King's health. Attempts to convert the RND to army practices were tried but were generally unsuccessful.

Service records for officers in the Royal Naval Division are in ADM 339/3, with the equivalent for ratings in ADM 339/1, although records of ratings who died on active service are in ADM 339/2.

The service records can be pretty informative, particularly for officers and for men killed in action. In all cases you will be given details of next-of-kin, date of birth and address, religion and civilian occupation, together with a physical description. Within the Division the card records movements and postings and, where appropriate, a date of when they were killed.

For men who died in service, the information is largely summarised in databases to the Division's casualties, which are on both Ancestry and Findmypast.

Further Reading

Geoffrey Sparrow and J. Macbean Ross, *On Four Fronts with the Royal Naval Brigade* (1918, republished 2011) – available through the Internet Archive

E.C. Coleman, *Khaki Jack: the Royal Naval Division in the First World War* (Amberley, 2014)

Identifying Military Uniforms

You may have photographs of the soldiers you are researching in uniform. As well providing a direct link to the past, the insignia and badges can tell you something about his service.

Officers and other ranks wore differently designed uniforms. It is always clear which was which. Officers' uniforms were better tailored and officers were rarely seen without a tie. Ordinary soldiers wore coarser tunics and trousers (kilts in the Highland regiments). Non-commissioned officers wore downward-pointing chevrons (one for a lance corporal, two for a corporal and three for a sergeant) on each arm above the elbow. They can be confused with long-service stripes found below the elbow.

Each regiment and corps had its own badge, worn on the cap or as buttons on the jacket and tunic. A few are very distinctive, such as the mounted gun for the Royal Artillery or the flaming grenade of the Grenadier Guards, but many are very similar.

There are various guides to help you. The best are Neil Storey, *Military Photographs and How to Date Them* (Countryside Books, 2010) and Robert Pols, *Identifying Old Army Photographs* (Family History Partnership, 2011). For regimental badges see Ian Swinnerton's *Identifying Your World War I Soldier from Badges and Photographs* (Family History Partnership, 2004) and Peter Doyle and Chris Foster's *British Army Cap Badges of the First World War* (Shire, 2010).

Probably the best general introduction to interpreting uniforms is provided by Chris McDonald at www.4thgordons.com/I-Spybook% 20of%20Uniforms1.2.pdf. There are several rather unsatisfactory sites to help identify regimental badges: the best is probably the British Armed Services and National Service site at www.britisharmed forces.org/index.php.

Gallantry Medals

Gallantry medals were awarded for acts of heroism and bravery on the field of battle. Some medals were awarded immediately for special acts (sometimes referred to as being awarded 'in the field'), while others – known as non-immediate – might be awarded weeks or months after the act.

The most prestigious gallantry medal is the Victoria Cross. Biographies of the 633 men who won the award during the First World War, together with descriptions of their exploits, are described by Gerald Gliddon in an excellent series of books published by The History Press, including *VCs of the First World War: Somme* (The History Press, 2011). There are also several websites devoted to VC winners, although Wikipedia, which has biographies of each man, is probably the best place to start. A register of VC winners can be found in series WO 98, together with copies of their citations, and other information is also available online on Discovery.

The Distinguished Service Order (DSO) was normally only awarded to senior officers, while the Military Cross (MC) was awarded for acts of bravery to officers of the rank of captain or below. The equivalents for non-commissioned officers and other ranks were the Distinguished Conduct Medal (DCM) and Military Medal (MM).

In many cases non-immediate gallantry awards were given out almost randomly to members of a platoon or company who had seen action. Often men were asked to nominate comrades who should be honoured.

If there isn't a family story about the award of a gallantry medal, or the medal itself, you may find a note on the Medal Index Card or, more rarely, in the service record.

Details of all gallantry awards were published in the *London Gazette*. For the higher awards there should be a citation that is a short description of why the medal was awarded. The citation for the Victoria Cross awarded to Captain William Henry Johnston, RE on 27 November 1914 reads:

> At Missy on 14th September under a heavy fire all day until 7 p.m., worked with his own hand two rafts bringing back wounded and returning with ammunition; thus enabling advanced Brigade to maintain its position across the river.

At the very least the *London Gazette* entry will give you the man's name, service number (not officers), rank, regiment and the date when the award was made. For awards of the Military Medal (MM) and Mentions in Despatches this is the only information you are likely to find.

However, it can be fairly hard to find anything else about how and why medals were won. The paperwork appears to have been destroyed during the Blitz. If you are lucky, you may be able to find something about the award of gallantry medals in the unit war diaries. Generally there are entries recording their award to officers and, less frequently, other ranks, without giving the reason why. You might also want to look at the brigade war diary of which the battalion was part, as awards had to be approved by the brigade's commanding officer.

Citations for awards of the Distinguished Conduct Medal (DCM) can be found on both Ancestry and Findmypast. They usually duplicate what appears in the *London Gazette,* but are certainly easier to find.

There are also some Medal Index Cards for men awarded the DCM and MM. They give you little more than the date and page number in the *London Gazette* where the award is listed. In my experience the date given is often wrong.

The Genealogist (www.thegenealogist.co.uk) has a set of cards of Military Medal winners, which give the date the award appeared in the *London Gazette*. Occasionally other information is given, such as the award of a second Military Medal ('a bar' in Army parlance). In addition, Findmypast has a list of artillerymen who won the Military Medal with the date their award was gazetted. In both cases the dates of publication in the *London Gazette* could be a few days out due to a backlog of entries waiting to be published.

The award of gallantry medals awards may well feature in newspaper stories.

The most common award was the Mention in Despatches (MiD) for acts of bravery or service that warranted reward, but were not enough to merit a gallantry award. During the First World War just over two per cent of the men in the British forces (141,082 officers and other ranks) were so honoured. Men are listed in the *London Gazette*. The fact that a man was awarded an MiD is usually shown on the Medal Index Card (often abbreviated to EM or EMB with a date when the award was published in the *Gazette*). There may also be separate cards with the approximate date the award was gazetted, although there are no other surviving records.

Further Reading

More about medals (both gallantry and campaign) can be found in Peter Duckers, *British Military Medals: a Guide for Collectors and Researchers* (2nd edition, Pen & Sword, 2013). Also useful is the *Medals Yearbook* published by Token Publishing annually and William Spencer, *Medals: the Researcher's Guide* (The National Archives, 2008).

Courts Martial

Some 300,000 soldiers and 6,000 officers faced courts martial during the First World War, generally for being absent without leave, petty theft or drunkenness. The Casualty Form in the service record will record misdemeanours and should indicate whether your ancestor was put on a charge. Registers of courts martial in WO 90 (for men serving overseas) and WO 92 (for men on home duty) give brief details of the offence. Details of more serious offences can be found in registers in WO 213, with a few files in WO 71 (including for those unfortunate men who were 'Shot at Dawn' for desertion and other offences) and WO 93.

Prisoners of War

Nearly 193,000 British and Commonwealth prisoners of war fell into the hands of the Germans and their allies during the war, about half of whom were captured during the last six months of the war. Conditions could be grim, generally because of increasing problems within Germany itself, rather than any deliberate policy to mistreat prisoners. Most prisoners came to rely on Red Cross parcels, which were collected and packed by voluntary organisations under the leadership of the British Red Cross.

The International Committee of the Red Cross (ICRC) in Geneva was responsible for passing details of prisoners of war between the various combatant nations and ensuring that conditions in the camps were adequate. The Committee collected, analysed and classified information it received from the detaining powers and national agencies about prisoners of war and civilian internees. It compared this information with requests submitted to it by relatives or friends, in order to restore contact between them. The Agency's collections consist of some 500,000 pages of lists and six million index cards, which can be extremely informative, although material for individual prisoners varies significantly. The records may tell you when and where a man was taken prisoner, the camps he was in and details of his next-of-kin back in Britain, perhaps when they were repatriated home or sent to Switzerland for recuperation. If they died while in German hands there may be a note about the date and place of death and where they were buried. For Rifleman Giles Eyre,

THE AUTHOR AS A PRISONER OF WAR, 1916

A photograph of Rifleman Giles Eyre, King's Royal Rifle Corps, taken soon after he was captured by the Germans during the Battle of the Somme. (Giles Eyr, *Somme Harvest: Memories of a PBI in the Summer of 1916 (1938)*)

2 King's Royal Rifle Corps, who was captured during the Battle of the Somme, they indicate that he was taken prisoner on 23 July at Contalmaison. By the end of August he appears on a list of men in the camp at Dülmen, where he presumably sat out the rest of the war. In his memoir *Somme Harvest: Memories of a PBI in the Summer of 1916* (published in 1938) he remembered sheltering overnight with a group of other soldiers in a shell hole near the German lines, when they were surprised by a German attack. In such situations it was not uncommon for both sides to kill their prisoners because of the difficulties of getting them back to their front lines. Fortunately for Rifleman Eyre, this didn't happen:

> Threatening faces closed around me and gestured and mouthed incoherencies. I moved forward hesitatingly to be instantly surrounded and pushed forward to the Hun trench. I went dazed and all at sea, my mind a seeking mass of emotions, my neck hurting like the very devil [he had been hit by a German rifle butt], and still grasping my rifle proceeded to clamber in, when with a snarl, a gigantic German thrust a pistol in my face and yelled 'Die Waffen runter! Schnell!' Luckily for myself I knew enough German to understand. Down went my rifle and quickly I dumped my equipment.

Through an intense British bombardment he was taken back through the German lines where he cursed his luck: 'The gods of chance had played us a scurvy trick…' However, to his surprise, he was well-treated by his captors.

In addition there are some reports about conditions in individual camps written in French or German. However, it is difficult to find out very much about individual POWs in British archives, as the records have largely been destroyed. A list of prisoners in German and Turkish hands in 1916 can be found in AIR 1/892/204/5/696-698 at Kew, which indicates where a prisoner was captured and when, where they were held and their next-of-kin. There is a published *List of Officers taken Prisoner in the Various Theatres of War between August 1914 and November 1918* (1919, reprinted 1988) online at Findmypast.

Returning British prisoners were interrogated by the authorities about their experiences and surviving reports (some 3,000 in total) can be downloaded from The National Archives website. Officers were interrogated about the circumstances of their capture and reports can be found in their service records.

Further Reading

Sarah Paterson, *Tracing Your First World War Prisoners of War* (Pen & Sword, 2012)
Richard van Emden, *Prisoners of the Kaiser* (Pen & Sword, 2009)

Pensions

Widows and disabled ex-servicemen were entitled to claim a pension. Much ill-feeling was created by the low level of the pension and the difficulties placed in the way of claimants by the government and local officials supervising the grant of awards. Most records have long since been destroyed. However, series PIN 82 at Kew contains an 8 per cent sample of widows' and dependents' papers, arranged in alphabetical order. The forms give personal details of each serviceman's name, place of residence, particulars of service and the date, place and cause of death or injury. They also give details of the assessment of, and entitlement to, pensions awards, the amount awarded, and the length of time for which the award was granted.

There is a set of post-First World War pension appeal records at the National Records of Scotland (www.nrscotland.gov.uk) in series PT6. The records contain detailed pension applications from thousands of Scottish soldiers and their next-of-kin (usually widows).

The Western Front Association (WFA) has a series of pension cards relating to the payment of pensions and other payments to soldiers and their dependents. As with all records of the First World War the content varies greatly between individuals, but you may expect to find material about the individual and his family as well as the reason why payments were made. At present the records are being indexed by the Association, but they will do look-ups for enquirers for a small fee. You can find out more at www.westernfrontassociation.com/great-war-current-news/pension-records.html.

Personal Papers and Effects

Soldiers (and indeed sailors and airmen) wrote about their war experiences in letters and diaries and many wrote up their memoirs in old age. An increasing number are appearing in print, on websites or in TV and radio programmes. That they did this is not surprising: they were witnessing events unique in human history.

There was a very efficient postal service. Most soldiers took advantage of this, scribbling regular letters home. Because of censorship, and not wanting to frighten their families, these letters tend to be fairly anodyne, reassuring the reader that they were well, perhaps indicating that they were safe behind the lines and asking for items to be sent out. In general they are not great works of literature, but even so, after nearly a century they are rightly treasured family heirlooms.

Neither officers nor men were allowed to keep diaries, although clearly many did. Some were just simple entries about the weather and where the soldier was stationed, in a pocket diary. Others were much more elaborate affairs.

Memoirs are also important. Some are based on diaries and letters, or correspondence with old comrades, while others were clearly written decades later for the grandchildren or to exorcise old ghosts.

You might have only a soldier's medals, army service discharge paper, pay book or photographs. Or no records at all, except vague family memories. If you do have a collection of records it is well worth considering donating them to the Imperial War Museum, or a local record office or regimental archive. They should be willing to give you a set of copies in return for the originals. Certainly you should think about making some provision for their care in your will.

There is no central list of what personal papers are to be found where, although it is worth checking TNA's Discovery Catalogue to see whether they have details of collections belonging to the soldier you are researching.

The Imperial War Museum has the most important collection of personal papers. In 2011 it had 17,500 separate collections of letters, diaries and memoirs, although not all relate to the First World War. Most collections are described in the museum's catalogue at www.iwm.org.uk/collections/search.

Another important resource is the Liddle Collection at Leeds University's Brotherton Library, which has over 4,000 collections of private papers. See http://library.leeds.ac.uk/liddle-collection.

Regimental archives and the National Army Museum are also good sources. The Royal Artillery Archives in Woolwich, for example, has extensive First World War collections, particularly for officers. In addition, small collections can sometimes be found at local record offices.

Lastly, an increasing number of diaries and memoirs in particular are being published or appearing online. Pen & Sword has published well over a hundred such titles, which you can buy direct at www.pen-and-sword.co.uk. Many others are available from the Naval and Military Press (www.naval-military-press.com). Some key titles are listed in the bibliography. A small selection is also at www.war-diary.com.

The Imperial War Museum and other museums have impressive collections of ephemera, which in the case of the IWM itself are included in its online catalogue. A small fraction is displayed in the impressive new galleries at the museum's London and Salford sites.

A fascinating Europe-wide initiative to collect personal items from each of the participating nations is being collated by Europeana at www.europeana1914-1918.eu/en. It brings home the often-forgotten fact that the war was fought by nations other than Britain and the British Empire.

The German Defences

John Masefield described the German defences which British troops faced as they crossed No Man's Land in July 1916.

The enemy wire was always deep, thick, and securely staked with iron supports, which were either crossed like the letter X, or upright, with loops to take the wire and shaped at one end like corkscrews so as to screw into the ground. The wire stood on these supports on a thick web, about four feet high and from thirty to forty feet across. The wire used was generally as thick as sailor's marline stuff, or two twisted rope-yarns. It contained, as a rule, some sixteen barbs to the foot. The wire used in front of our lines was generally galvanized, and remained grey after months of exposure. The enemy wire, not being galvanized, rusted to a black colour, and shows up black at a great distance. In places this web or barrier was supplemented with trip-wire, or wire placed just above the ground, so that the artillery observing officers might not see it and so not cause it to be destroyed. This trip-wire was as difficult to cross as the wire of the entanglements. In one place (near the Y Ravine at Beaumont-Hamel) this trip-wire was used with thin iron spikes a yard long of the kind known as caltrops. The spikes were so placed in the ground that about one foot of spike projected. The scheme was that our men should catch their feet in the trip-wire, fall on the spikes, and be transfixed.

In places, in front of the front line in the midst of his wire, sometimes even in front of the wire, the enemy had carefully hidden snipers and machine-gun posts. Sometimes these outside posts were connected with his front-line trench by tunnels, sometimes they were simply shell-holes, slightly altered with a spade to take the snipers and the gunners...

When these places had been passed, and the enemy wire, more or less cut by our shrapnel, had been crossed, our men had to attack the enemy fire trenches of the first line. These, like the other defences, varied in degree, but not in kind. They were, in the main, deep, solid trenches, dug with short bays or zigzags in the pattern of the Greek Key or a badger's earth. They were seldom less than eight feet and sometimes as much as twelve feet deep. Their sides were revetted, or held from collapsing, by strong wickerwork. They had good, comfortable standing slabs or banquettes on which the men could stand to fire. As a rule, the parapets were not built up with sandbags as ours were.

In some parts of the line, the front trenches were strengthened at intervals of about fifty yards by tiny forts or fortlets [pillboxes] made of concrete and so built into the parapet that they could not be seen from without, even five yards away. These fortlets were pierced with a foot-long slip for the muzzle of a machine gun, and were just big enough to hold the gun and one gunner.

In the forward wall of the trenches were the openings of the shafts which led to the frontline dugouts. The shafts are all of the same pattern. They have open mouths about four feet high, and slant down into the earth for about twenty feet at an angle of forty-five degrees. At the bottom of the stairs which led down are the living rooms and barracks which communicate with each other so that if a shaft collapses the men below may still escape by another. The shafts and living rooms are strongly propped and panelled with wood, and this has led to the destruction of most of the few which survived our bombardment. While they were needed as billets our men lived in them. Then the wood was removed, and the dugout and shaft collapsed.

During the bombardment before an attack, the enemy kept below in his dugouts. If one shaft were blown in by a shell, they passed to the next. When the fire 'lifted' to let the attack begin, they raced up the stairs with their machine guns and had them in action within a minute. Sometimes the fire was too heavy for this, for trench, parapet, shafts, dugouts, wood, and fortlets, were pounded out of existence, so that no man could say that a line had ever run there; and in these cases the garrison was destroyed in the shelters. This happened in several places, though all the enemy dugouts were kept equipped with pioneer tools by which buried men could dig themselves out...

The enemy batteries were generally placed behind banks or lynchets which gave good natural cover; but in many places he mounted guns in strong permanent emplacements, built up of timber balks, within a couple of miles (at Fricourt within a quarter of a mile) of his front line. In woods from the high trees of which he could have clear observation, as in the Bazentin, Bernafay, and Trônes Woods, he had several of these emplacements, and also stout concrete fortlets for heavy single guns...

Our attacks were met by a profuse machine gun fire from the trench parapets and from the hidden pits between and outside the lines. There was not very much rifle fire in any part of the battle, but all the hotly fought for strongholds were defended by machine guns to the last. It was reported that the bodies of some enemy soldiers were found chained to their guns, and that on the bodies of others were intoxicating pills, designed to madden and infuriate the takers before an attack. The fighting in the trenches was mainly done by bombing with hand-grenades, of which the enemy had several patterns, all effective. His most used type was a grey tin cylinder, holding about a pound of explosive, and screwed to a wooden baton or handle about a foot long for the greater convenience of throwing.

Taken from John Masefield, *The Old Front Line* (1917)

Chapter 3

CASUALTIES

Commonwealth War Graves Commission

Just over 700,000 British men and several hundred women were killed during the First World War and many hundreds of thousands more received some form of medical treatment. Some 150,000 British and Commonwealth men died in or around the Somme, of whom just over half have no known grave. These men are commemorated on the majestic memorial to the missing at Thiepval. About 80 per cent of the casualties occurred during the Battle of the Somme; that is between 1 July and 10 November 1916. And perhaps another 100,000 fell elsewhere in France and are commemorated in hundreds of cemeteries large and small.

The gravestone for Capt R. J. McCoughlin, who is buried in the cemetery at Vendresse near Laon, showing the epitaph chosen by his family. (*Author*)

Every British and Commonwealth soldier who died during the First World War is marked in some way by the Commonwealth War Graves Commission. The Commission was set up in May 1917 to remember the dead of the First World War. It was decided early in the war that no bodies would be brought back to Britain, so that they would lie with their fallen comrades. A total of approximately 411,600 men have named graves in France and Belgium; there are some 158,700 other graves which contain men whose bodies could not be identified with certainty, and the names of 313,700 are

35

listed in Memorials to the Missing, principally on the huge memorials at Ypres and Tyne Cot (both in Belgium) and Thiepval.

Regardless of rank the gravestones contain the same information: name, rank, service number, unit, decorations, date of death and age. There is the unit badge for the unit the man was serving with when he was killed, an emblem of religious faith (generally a cross), and occasionally a personal inscription chosen by the next-of-kin. At a cost of three pence halfpenny per character (up to a maximum of 66 characters including spaces), a family could have an inscription added to the grave, but as it was expensive relatively few gravestones have inscriptions. Most are just quotes from the Bible or lines from poetry, but in almost every cemetery there are one or two with more imaginative inscriptions. On Sgt John William Streets' stone at Euston Road Cemetery at Colincamps the inscription reads: 'I FELL BUT YIELDED NOT MY ENGLISH SOUL'.

At St Sever Cemetery, the inscription of 2/Lt Gordon Minter Freake, 1/4th Oxfordshire and Buckinghamshire Light Infantry, who was killed on 1 August 1916 aged 19, reads 'JOINED 1914 I HAVE ONLY DONE MY DUTY HAVE NO REGRETS FOR RESULT SICKLE TRENCH POZIERES 1916'. In the same cemetery lies Lt Anthony Percival, 9th Machine Gun Corps, killed 25 October 1917, aged 25 'TONY AND LEILA'S DARLING ONLY CHILD LOVED AND MOURNED BY MANY'. At Beaumont-Hamel British Cemetery the inscription for Sgt Norman Blissett, 1st Hampshire Regiment, who was among the nearly 20,000 men who were killed on 1 July 1916, must sum up the sentiments of many grieving families 'YOUTH HAD SCARCELY WRITTEN HIS NAME ON HER PAGE'.

Even today bodies are still being recovered from the fields and woods in which they fell and are reburied with military honours. The most famous recent example of this was at Fromelles, where the bodies of 250 Australian and British soldiers who were killed on 19 and 20 July 1916 were found in a local wood in 2009 and reburied in 2010. There is now an excellent small museum at the cemetery explaining how the bodies were recovered and subsequently identified (for more details see Chapter 8).

The Commission is perhaps best known for the hundreds of carefully tended, and very moving, cemeteries scattered through northern France and Belgium, although it maintains cemeteries in 150 countries across the

Soldiers Died in the Great War

Additional information can often be found in the Soldiers Died in the Great War databases available through both Ancestry and Findmypast. The War Office originally compiled these records in the early 1920s. Soldiers Died contains more details than those provided by the Commonwealth War Graves Commission, notably including the place and date of enlistment and home address.

Information listed about an individual may include: name, rank and number; birthplace; where they enlisted; home town; regiment and battalion; type of casualty; date of death and theatre of war where the individual died, generally Western Europe. Occasionally a place of death is also given. The cause of a man's death is also provided, which can be a useful clue in working out how it occurred. Almost always this is Killed in Action – that is during the fighting itself – or Died of Wounds – that is in a casualty clearing station or hospital behind the lines. If he was killed in action then it is worth checking the war diary to see whether there is additional information.

War Diaries

War diaries are a daily record of events compiled by infantry battalions and other units. The originals are at The National Archives in series WO 95. For more about Unit War Diaries see Chapter 6.

Inevitably, casualties are often mentioned. Normally entries just baldly state the numbers. The war diary for the Accrington Pals (11th East Lancashire), written at 1am on 2 July 1916 (WO 95/2366) records casualties as being 'Officers killed 7, missing 1, wounded 13 including the Commanding Officer. Other ranks killed 86, wounded 338, missing 140.'

The deaths of individual officers may be recorded. The entry at noon in the war diary for the Sheffield City Battalion (12th York and Lancaster Regiment) on 1 July 1916 indicates that the following officers had already been killed: Captain W.A. Colley, Captain W.S. Clark, 2nd Lieut. C.H. Wardill and 2nd Lieutenant E.M. Carr. (WO 95/2365).

It is much rarer to find the names of individual privates or non-commissioned officers. But it does happen. Irish regiments are particularly good at providing lists of casualties in their war diaries.

The entry for John Manson Sandison in the roll of honour compiled for men from the Shetland Islands who had served in the Great War.

Died at Rouen on Feb. 28. 1917, from wounds received in action at Miraumont, on the Ancre. Aged 25 years.

JOHN MANSON SANDISON.

Private, Seaforth Highlanders. Son of Andrew and Mary Sandison, Sandwick, Hillswick. Killed by a shell at Gouzeaucourt, on 7th August, 1917. Aged 21 years.

SKAL·LAND BYGGIA·

Unusual deaths may be recorded: the diary for the 1st Honourable Artillery Company for 11 October 1916 (WO 95/3118/1) notes that 'Pte Freeman A.D. was killed [...] his kitten which he carried as a mascot was asleep on his chest, unhurt, when he was found.' Twenty-two-year-old Pte Alfred Dyson Freeman of Peckham is buried at Mailly-Maillet Communal Cemetery Extension.

You may be able to work out the circumstances of a man's death even if he is not explicitly named, particularly if it was an isolated death. Privates John Manson Sandison, from Shetland, and Arbroath's William Duncan, of the 7th Seaforth Highlanders, were killed on 7 August 1917. They were in a quiet sector of the front at Havrincourt. The entry in the war diary for the day (WO 95/1765/4) records:

Some rain and mist, consequently very quiet and possible to move and work in the open. Enemy got a direct hit on left ('D' Coy) firing live at 7pm with a 5.9 [shell] killing 2 and wounding 3 OR.

Duncan and Sandison were the only casualties during the tour of duty that had begun on 2 August. Much of the time was spent repairing the trench walls and installing latrines. Ironically, the battalion was due to be relieved later that evening. The two men lie next to each other in Ruyaulcourt Military Cemetery near Bapaume. One wonders whether they were friends in life.

Missing in Action

If you are researching an individual for whom there is no known grave it is worth seeing whether his disappearance was reported to the International Committee of the Red Cross in Geneva. If it was, there may

---

The Missing of the Somme Database

Pam and Ken Linge's life work has been to create a database about the men who were posted as being missing during battles on the Somme, and who are commemorated on the Thiepval memorial. The database, which can only be searched at the memorial's visitor centre, contains a huge amount of information about nearly 10,000 men. Photographs of some of the missing appear on a montage in the foyer. More information can be found at www.telegraph.co.uk/news/uknews/8124065/Armistice-Day-on-the-trail-of-the-Missing.html. Mr and Mrs Linge are always looking for new material, so if you can help their email is pam_ken.linge@btinternet.com and their postal address is: Drystones, Heugh House Lane, Haydon Bridge, Northumberland, NE47 6HJ. They have also written a book based on their researches, *Missing but Not Forgotten: Men of the Thiepval Memorial – Somme* (Pen & Sword, 2015)

They are unable to do any research for enquirers.

be a card for him, which will provide details of when and where he was reported missing, his unit and the company he was in, together with details of next-of-kin. Occasionally there may be a note of his fate, whether he survived to become a prisoner of war or died of wounds while in German hands. These records are online at http://grande guerre.icrc.org. Armed with this information then you can turn to the war diaries for a description of how and why he went missing.

Soldiers' Effects

Ancestry has digitised registers of the effects of men who were killed in action or died of wounds. At first look they are of little interest, but often you will find exact details of a man's unit and perhaps the hospital he was at when he died. There are also notes about the payment of sums to the individual's next-of-kin. Pte Alfred Dixon (not Dyson) Freeman left just over £5, which went to his sister and her family.

Also worth looking out for (and still rather moving) are lists of a man's personal possessions that were returned to the family. Men were expected to leave anything personal behind in special lockers before they went into the front line. These are routinely found in service records of deceased officers and I have come across them occasionally in soldiers' records as well.

Casualty Lists

From the beginning of the war the War Office published daily lists of casualties, both lists of men killed and those wounded. The lists of deaths in particular were picked up by many newspapers. Even if a man returned home the Lists are worth checking, just in case he was recorded as wounded.

The information given is basic, just name, rank and unit, together with home town. No dates are given for when a man was killed or wounded, but you can assume that the events took place four to six weeks before the information was published in the Casualty Lists. John Mayberry, of the Connaught Rangers, is noted as being wounded in the List of 13 January 1915, which is probably the reason why he was discharged as being unfit for service eighteen months later, but where he was wounded and what happened has long been forgotten.

The four to six week rule is of course only a rough guide. John William Streets, who was killed on 1 July 1916, is announced as being wounded and missing on 13 September 1916, but it was over a year before his death was confirmed on 20 September 1917.

An incomplete set of Lists is available on *The Genealogist* and many were published in *The Times* and other newspapers.

Rolls of Honour

One phenomenon of the war was the roll of honour: a published list of the deceased (and occasionally other groups of servicemen such as prisoners of war). Rolls are often available for workplaces (such as local councils and railway companies), chapels and small communities. They are definitely worth looking out for, although in most cases the information they contain can easily be obtained from the Commonwealth War Graves Commission or Soldiers Died in the Great War databases.

There is no nationwide set of these rolls, although the Imperial War Museum and British Library almost certainly have the largest collections. A good many are with the Society of Genealogists in London. Archives and local study libraries may have copies of rolls for their area. A number have been republished by the Naval and Military Press (www.naval-military-press.com). Many Scottish ones are available online through the Internet Archive (www.archive.org) courtesy of the National Library of Scotland. Others are on the Roll of Honour website (www.roll-of-honour.com), but not all rolls are online by any means.

A fine example is the Shetland Roll of Honour, which was originally published in 1920 and is now available on the Internet Archive. Great care was taken to contact all the islanders to ensure that all the information was accurate. It lists all the men from the Islands who served in HM forces. As might be expected, most Shetlanders joined the Royal Navy, but a surprising number enlisted in the Army. There are also more details and photographs for each of the men who fell. Each page is handsomely decorated with scenes of local life and landscape. For John Manson Sandison the Roll indicates he was the son of Andrew and Mary Sandison

FIRST-AID ON THE BATTLE-FIELD: A CAMERA IMPRESSION ON THE SOMME FRONT. [British official photograph.]
Wounded soldiers undergoing quick but expert treatment at an advanced dressing-station. As soon as their immediate needs were satisfied the motor-ambulance conveyed them to the base hospital. On the horizon the smoke of a bursting shell can be distinctly seen.

An advanced dressing station on the Somme. These stations were where wounded men would receive basic medical treatment before being passed down the line to casualty clearing stations and base hospitals. (*Wellcome Library*)

of Sandwick, Hardwick and that: 'He was killed by a shell at Gouzeaucourt'. John was aged twenty-one when he died.

There are several larger national rolls. Entries for some 26,000 officers and other ranks (including 7,000 photographs) were collected and published in 1917 by the Marquis Melville de Ruvigny, a noted genealogist of the period. De Ruvigny's 'Roll of Honour: A Biographical Record of His Majesty's Military and Aerial Forces Who Fell in the Great War 1914–1917' is available on Ancestry and Findmypast.

If you are researching Irish soldiers it is worth looking at Ireland's Memorial Records of the Great War which is available on Ancestry, the Naval and Military Archive and Findmypast's Irish website, www.find mypast.ie.

Medical Records

If the service record survives it should contain a Casualty Form (Form B103), which records visits to the doctor, admission to hospital and so on. Of course many entries do detail war-related wounds, but a surprising number of entries concern normal ailments and complaints. The forms can sometimes be difficult to decode because, as we have seen, they also contain details of postings, promotions and demotions, as well as punishments.

The Royal Army Medical Corps (RAMC) was responsible for medical care and the provision of decent sanitation. A man's chances of survival depended on how quickly his wound was treated. The whole process was designed to achieve this as efficiently as possible.

Closest to the front line was the Regimental Aid Post (RAP) run by the battalion medical officer; his orderlies and stretcher-bearers, attended these. The medical officer was embedded in the battalion and came from the Royal Army Medical Corps (RAMC). There would also be a sergeant or corporal and perhaps one or two other ranks from the Corps. The quality of medical officers varied tremendously: some were excellent,

The entry for Sgt William Caldwell, 21st Northumberland Fusiliers, in the Hospital Records. He recovered from his gunshot wound to be discharged in 1919. (*Forces War Records/The National Archives*)

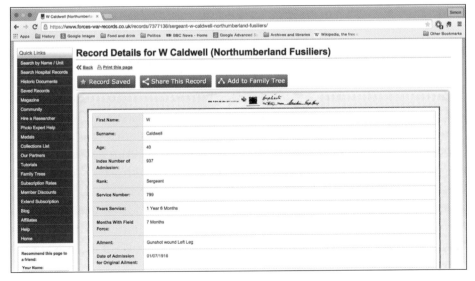

while others were so poor that soldiers avoided seeing them unless they absolutely had to. The MO was also responsible for public health and ensuring that sanitation met the required standards. This was important work, if often overlooked, but it ensured that there were few outbreaks of malaria, dysentery or enteric fever, which had debilitated so many men in previous wars.

In action, the RAP was situated a few metres behind the front line. The RMO was helped by the regimental stretcher-bearers, who traditionally were also the regimental bandsmen.

The facilities were only sufficient to carry out first aid. The object of the exercise was to patch them up and either return them to their duties in the line, or pass them back to an Advance Dressing Station (ADS).

In battle a casualty was to be transported direct to the ADS, but to avoid congestion Collecting Posts (CPs) and Relay Posts (RPs) were sometimes set up. This meant there were teams of RAMC stretcher bearers, strung out over miles of ground unpassable by motor or horse transport, shuttling between the posts and passing the wounded on to the next team. A 'carry' could be anything up to four miles over muddy or shell-pocked ground, either in trenches or above ground.

There was at least one, but normally two, Advanced Dressing Stations set up by the Field Ambulances. Ideally, the Advance Dressing Station would be sited about 400 yards behind the RAPs, in tents where necessary, but preferably in large houses or schools, with the Main Dressing Station (MDS) sited a mile or so further back.

The Field Ambulance was the most forward of the RAMC units. Each brigade had a Field Ambulance assigned to it. When the brigade was out of the line the units were allocated special tasks such providing a scabies centre or, for other ailments, a Divisional Rest Centre (DRS), or bath unit.

An Infantry Field Ambulance comprised ten officers and 182 other ranks from the RAMC. In each Field Ambulance there was a Headquarters Company (A Section) who made up the Main Dressing Station and two Sections (B and C Coy) which formed the two ADSs. Each section was further sub-divided into the 'tent division' who were the medical staff and formed the treatment area, and the 'bearers' who collected the casualties from the RAPs and carried them back to the 'tent division' at the ADS, or manned the relay posts.

The ADS were meant to provide sufficient treatment so the men could be quickly returned to their units where possible. If the casualty was not fit enough, he was sent to the Casualty Clearing Station (CCS). Later in the war fully equipped surgical teams were attached to the Field Ambulances.

The Casualty Clearing Stations facilitated movement of casualties from the battlefield to the hospitals. They were very large units, with a minimum of fifty beds and 150 stretchers in order to treat a minimum of 200 sick and wounded at any one time. In normal circumstances the team would be made up of seven medical officers, one quartermaster and seventy-seven other ranks; there would also be a dentist, a pathologist, seven nurses and other non-medical personnel including VADs.

CCSs were usually situated about 20 kilometres behind the front lines, roughly midway between the front line and the Base Area, and about 500 yards from a main railway line or waterway system. This was the first line of surgery and as close as the nursing staff would get to the front line. Even so treatment was still only limited.

CCSs collected casualties from the ADSs by using Motor Ambulance Convoy. Each ambulance had an ASC driver and an RAMC attendant. Men would stay up to four weeks in order to recover before they returned to their units or were transferred by Ambulance Trains or Inland Water Transport to a hospital. The limited medical aid available meant that many men died, which is why the locations of many CCSs are marked by cemeteries.

There were two Stationary Hospitals to every Division and each one was designed to hold up to 400 casualties. There was, however, a tendency to use these as specialist hospitals, i.e. sick; VD; gas victims, neurasthenia cases, epidemics and so on. They normally occupied what had been a civilian hospital.

A General Hospital was located on or near railway lines to facilitate movement of casualties from the Casualty Clearing Stations on to the ports. Hotels and other large buildings such as casinos were requisitioned, but other hospitals were hutted and constructed on open ground. In Base Areas such as Etaples and Boulogne General Hospitals had all the facilities of normal civilian hospitals. Men would stay until they were either fully fit or they were sent back to Britain for specialist care or to recuperate from their wounds.

This section is based on the web page 'Chain of Evacuation' on the RAMC website www.ramc-ww1.com/chain_of_evacuation.php. More about the care of the wounded can be found, with lists of where many of the hospitals were based, at www.1914-1918.net/wounded.htm.

An efficient system of dealing with casualties was quickly introduced on the outbreak of war to ferry the sick and wounded to the appropriate Casualty Clearing Station or hospital in the rear. A card was compiled for each man, but all these records (with the exception of a small sample) have long been destroyed. A very limited selection of records is in series MH 106 at The National Archives and online with Forces War Records.

If you know which hospital a soldier was in when he returned to Britain, it may also be worth checking the online database of hospital records (www.nationalarchives.gov.uk/hospitalrecords) to see whether anything survives at local archives or with the hospital itself.

Sue Light has an excellent guide to medical records at www.scarlet finders.co.uk/125.htm.

Silver War Badge

The Silver War Badge was instituted in 1916. It was a small, circular lapel badge made of sterling silver, which bore the king's initials, a crown, and the inscriptions 'For King and Empire' and 'Services Rendered'. All in all just over a million badges were issued. The badge provided former soldiers with some form of identification to show that they had faithfully served King and Country. Not all ex-servicemen applied, but where they did the forms, which are on Ancestry, will tell you when a man enlisted and was discharged, the particular unit he was serving with at the date of discharge (particularly useful for sappers and gunners as it may be the only clue you get to the unit they were with) and occasionally the reason for discharge. More often the entry just says 'wounds' or 'sick', with a reference to the appropriate part of paragraph 392 of the King's Regulations (see opposite).

Criteria for Discharge

On service records, medal index cards and the registers of the Silver War Badge you may come across a set of abbreviations, perhaps something like K.R. 392 (xvi). This refers to paragraph 392 of the 1912 edition of the King's Regulations, which governed how the British Army was to be administered. The paragraph contained all the official causes of discharge, which were set out in a series of sub-paragraphs. The vast majority of men who applied for the badge were discharged in respect of sub-paragraph xvi, as being 'No longer physically fit for war service', although by 1917 you may find skilled men whose skills were considered more use in the war effort at home rather than in the trenches.

The criteria for discharge were:

(i)   References on enlistment being unsatisfactory

(ii)   Having been irregularly enlisted

(iii)   Not likely to become an efficient soldier, (with sub clauses as below)

    (a)   Recruit rejected both by Medical Officer and Approving Officer

    (b)   Recruit passed by Medical Officer, but rejected by a Recruiting Officer stationed away from the headquarters of the recruiting area, or by Approving Officer

    (c)   Recruit within three months of enlistment considered unfit for service

    (cc) Recruits with more than three months' service considered unfit for further military service

    (d)   Recruit who after having undergone a course of physical training is recommended by an examining board to be discharged, or in the case of a mounted corps is unable to ride

    (e)   Soldier of local battalion abroad considered unlikely to become efficient

    (f)   Boy who, on reaching 18 years of age, is considered to be physically unfit for the ranks

(iv)	Having been claimed as an apprentice
(v)	Having claimed it on payment of £10 within three months of his attestation
(vi)	Having made a mis-statement as to age on enlistment (with sub clauses as below)
	(a) Soldier under 17 years of age at date of application for discharge
	(b) Soldier between 17 and 18 years of age at date of application for discharge
(vii)	Having been claimed for wife desertion (with sub clauses as below)
	(a) By the parish authorities
	(b) By the wife
(viii)	Having made a false answer on attestation
(ix)	Unfitted for the duties of the corps
(x)	Having been convicted by the civil power of a specific offence, such as rape or murder, or of an offence committed before enlistment
(xi)	For misconduct
(xii)	Having been sentenced to penal servitude
(xiii)	Having been sentenced to be discharged with ignominy
(xiv)	At his own request, on payment of a specified amount under Article 1130 (i), Pay Warrant
(xv)	Free, after a specific number of years' service under Article 1130 (ii), Pay Warrant (with sub clauses as below)
(xva)	Free under Article 1130 (i), Pay Warrant
(xvb)	Free to take up civil employment which cannot be held open
(xvi)	No longer physically fit for war service
(xvia)	Surplus to military requirements (having suffered impairment since entry into the service)
(xvii)	*– paragraph not used*
(xviii)	At his own request after 18 years' service (with a view to pension under the Pay Warrant)
(xix)	For the benefit of the public service after 18 years' service (with a view to pension under the Pay Warrant)

(xx)	Inefficiency after 18 years' service (with a view to pension under the Pay Warrant)
(xxi)	The termination of his period of engagement
(xxii)	With less than 21 years' service towards engagement, but with 21 or more years' service towards pension
(xxiii)	Having claimed discharge after three months' notice
(xxiv)	Having reached the age for discharge
(xxv)	His services being no longer required
	(a) Surplus to military requirements (Not having suffered impairment since entry into the service)
(xxvi)	At his own request after 21 (or more) years' service (with a view to pension under the Pay Warrant)
(xxvii)	After 21 (or more) years' qualifying service for pension, and with 5 (or more) years' service as warrant officer (with a view to pension under the Pay Warrant)
(xxxviii)	On demobilisation

At Le Cateau

Reservist Frank Richards rejoined the 2nd Royal Welch Fusiliers on the declaration of war and soon found himself in France.

About ten yards from the side of the road was a straw rick, and about half a dozen men had got down the other side of it. I slipped over and woke them up. One man we had a job with but we got him going at last. By this time the Company had moved off, so we were stragglers. We came to some crossroads and didn't know which way to go. Somehow we decided to take the road to the right. Dawn was now breaking. Along the road we took were broken-down motor lorries, motorcycles, dead horses and broken wagons.

In a field were dumped a lot of rations. We had a feed, crammed some biscuits into our haversacks and moved along again. After a few minutes, by picking up more stragglers, we were twenty strong, men of several different battalions. I inquired if anyone had seen the 2nd Royal Welch Fusiliers, but nobody had. By the time that it was full daylight there were thirty-five of us marching along, including two sergeants.

We got into a small village—I had long since lost interest in the names of the places we came to, so I don't know where it was—where we met a staff-officer who took charge of us. He marched us out of the village and up a hill and told us to extend ourselves in skirmishing order at two paces interval and lie down and be prepared to stop an attack at any moment. About five hundred yards in front of us was a wood, and the attack would come from that direction. The enemy commenced shelling our position, but the shells were falling about fifteen yards short. The man on my left was sleeping: he was so dead-beat that the shelling didn't worry him in the least and the majority of us were not much better. We lay there for about half an hour but saw no signs of the enemy.

The staff-officer then lined us up and told us to attach ourselves to the first battalion we came across. I had to shake and thump the man on my left before I could wake him up. We marched off again and came across lots of people who had left their homes. Four ladies in an open carriage insisted on getting out to let some of our crippled and dead-beat men have a ride. We packed as many as we could into the carriage and moved along, the ladies marching with us. Late in the afternoon we took leave of the ladies. The men who had been riding had a good day's rest and sleep. If the ladies had all our wishes they would be riding in a Rolls-Royce for the rest of their lives.

During the evening when passing through a village I got news that the Battalion had passed through it an hour before. I and a man named Rhodes decided to leave the band and try and catch them up. During the next few days we attached ourselves to three different battalions, but immediately left them when we got news of our own. We wandered on for days, living on anything we could scrounge. It seemed to us that trying to find the Battalion was like trying to chase a will-o'- the wisp. But we were going the right way. All roads seemed to lead to Paris...

The following day we came to a railhead. A train was in and an officer inquired if we had lost our unit. We said that we had, so he ordered us to get into the train, which was full of troops who were in the same fix as ourselves. No one knew where we were going to, but we all believed that we were going to Paris. One battalion that we had been with had been told by their officers that they were going to Paris for a rest. Everybody seemed to have Paris on the brain. We had a long train journey and I slept the greater part of the way.

We detrained at a place called Le Mans. The only thing I can remember about this place was a large French barracks where we stayed and a street named after one of the Wright brothers of aeroplane fame. I expect I was too dulled with marching to notice anything more. We were there about a week and then got sent up country again. We picked the Battalion up just after they had passed through Coulommiers.

I could not find Billy or Stevens; when I asked what had become of them I was told that Stevens had been missing after the Battalion left St Quentin. Then a man named Slavin said that Billy and himself had left the Battalion about fifteen miles from Paris. Billy had a touch of fever. They had got a lift in a motor lorry into Paris where Billy was admitted into hospital. Slavin said that he had stayed in Paris for four days and the last day he was there he saw Billy riding in a grand motor car with two French ladies; the way Billy waved his hand to him, anyone would have thought he was a bloody lord. Billy was lucky enough to be sent home, and I never saw him again.

Frank Richards, *Old Soldiers Never Die* (Faber & Faber, 1933)

Chapter 4

WOMEN IN FRANCE

As well as men thousands of British and Commonwealth women saw service in France as nurses, clerks and in other trades. However, so far as is known none went into the trenches, apart from the rather special case of Dorothy Lawrence, who enlisted into the Royal Engineers as Sapper Dennis Smith.

Despite their contribution to the war effort, there are relatively few records for women. And before you start you have to have a rough idea at least about your ancestor's war service.

Some records for women are identical to those for men. In particular, women who served overseas either in the forces or as volunteers in hospitals or canteens were entitled to the same campaign medals as men. Details of these awards can be found in the Medal Index Cards (and Medal Rolls) in the same way you would research a soldier or sailor. The information given is identical, although it is generally not terribly helpful. However, Ancestry's set does not include women recipients, so you must use those on The National Archives website.

The appointment, promotion, and resignation of officers in the nursing services and auxiliary corps should be recorded in the *London Gazette*. In addition, the *Gazette* will record the award of gallantry medals to women (generally the Royal Red Cross and Mentions in Despatches).

Several thousand women were killed on active service. They are commemorated in the normal way by the Commonwealth War Graves Commission. In addition many Army workers, nurses and VADs are listed in Soldiers Died in Great War, including some who died in Britain.

Nurses

By the middle of 1917 some 45,000 nurses were serving in the armed forces and thousands more women were doing auxiliary work in hospitals at home and in France. Edward Liveing, who was wounded on

Nurses assist in a operating theatre behind the Somme battlefield. (*Wellcome Library*)

1 July 1916, remembered being treated at a Casualty Clearing Station: 'There were two Army nurses at work on a case next to mine – the first English women I had seen since I returned from leave six months before.'

Before the war Queen Alexandra's Imperial Military Nursing Service (QAIMNS) had maintained small nursing services, which greatly expanded during the war.

Service records for Army nurses, including members of the Territorial Force Nursing Service, are online on The National Archives website. The records can tell you where a nurse trained; references relating to their suitability as military nurses; which hospitals, Field Ambulances, Casualty Clearing Stations or other medical units they served in; confidential reports about their performance, and when they left the services.

Nurses could be awarded the Royal Red Cross for meritorious service. The Royal Red Cross was created in 1883 by Queen Victoria, as an award to nursing sisters or women for outstanding service in the care of the sick or wounded of the armed services. Just over 6,700 awards were made during the First World War, but often to administrators rather than nurses near the front.

This decoration had two classes, first class (members) with the post-nominal letters RRC, and second class (associates) ARRC. Awards were announced in the *London Gazette* and there are registers in series WO 145, but they may not tell you anything you haven't already gleaned from the *London Gazette*, except the person who presented the medal, where and the date it happened. Using the information it may be worth seeing whether there was a story in the local newspaper about its presentation.

Findmypast has a small database of military nurses who were active in the early twentieth century, including some 1,600 volunteers who served with the Scottish Women's Hospital.

Voluntary Aid Detachments (VADs)

The British Red Cross Society and the Order of St John had, in 1909, set up a nationwide network of Voluntary Aid Detachments (VADs), comprising men and women who would help in hospitals and provide other assistance on the outbreak of war. These people became known as VADs.

The nursing assistants – VADs – had a mixed reputation. In general they were badly treated by nurses and doctors, when not ignored altogether. Edie Appelton, an experienced Army nurse, wrote in her diary for 29 November 1915:

> The V.A.D.s are a source of great interest to me – taking them as a bunch they are splendid. They may be roughly divided into 4 sorts: 'Stalkers', 'Crawlers', the irresponsible butterflyers and the sturdy pushers.
>
> At the moment I am thinking of a butterfly one who is on night duty in these wards and says with a light hearted laugh: 'It's rippin' nursin' the men, great fun, when I was in the Officers' ward I did housework all the time, great fun – but there men are really ill – great fun.' When I show her how to do anything fresh, she twitches to get at it and says 'oh do let me try, I'd love to do that, simply love to.' She is an aristocratic little person most dainty and well groomed and the thought of her doing scrubbing and dusting all day – makes me smile.

VADs were members either of the British Red Cross Society or the Order of St John. Both organisations kept record cards for individuals, which may include the dates of service, the nature of the duties performed, the detachment the individual belonged to, the institutions and places where the individual served, and any honours that may have been awarded. In addition, there are indexes for personnel who served in military hospitals, who were trained nurses, and who received the campaign medals. Brief details of all VADs are online at www.redcross.org.uk/About-us/Who-we-are/History-and-origin/First-World-War. You can also request a copy of a record card from the Red Cross.

Further reading

Sue Light's superb Scarlet Finders website www.scarletfinders.co.uk/index.html has lots about military nursing during the two world wars, with an emphasis on the First World War. She also writes a fascinating blog on nurses of the First World War at http://greatwarnurses.blogspot.com.

Auxiliary Corps

The Royal Navy in 1916 was the first service to recruit women, who became cooks, clerks, wireless telegraphists, code experts and electricians, although it was not until November 1917 that a separate Women's Royal Naval Service (WRNS) was set up. The Army noted the success of the Navy's experiment and rather nervously established the Women's Army Auxiliary Corps (WAAC, later Queen Mary's Auxiliary Army Corps QMAAC) in March 1917 to undertake similar work, thus releasing men for the front.

The first members of the Corps arrived in France on 31 March 1917. Fourteen women, led by Miss F.W. Findlay, arrived at Boulogne, spending the night at the RFC club for officers at Abbeville. Apart from nurses they were the first British women to enter a war zone in official uniform. The clerks, and the women who soon joined them, were kept well away from any actual fighting, and, so far as was humanly possible, from young men in general. Their arrival in France was the final acceptance of the importance of women's contribution to the war effort. As female

Lady ambulance drivers with their vehicles at Etaples in November 1918. In the last eighteen months of the war women increasingly took over the work of men, releasing them for service at the front. (*Wellcome Library*)

journalist F. Tennyson Jesse later wrote: 'The thing was no longer a game at which women were making silly asses of themselves and pretending to be men; it had become regular, ordered, disciplined and worthy of respect. In short, uniform was no longer fancy dress.'

WAAC

The WAAC was divided into four sections: Cookery; Mechanical; Clerical and Miscellaneous. Most stayed on the Home Front, but around 9,000 served in France and Flanders. The grades (ranks) were divided into Controllers and Administrators (officers) and Members (other ranks). Within the Members there were forewomen (sergeants), assistant forewomen (corporals) and workers (privates). Inevitably, a member was still paid less than a man in the Army doing the same work. The WAAC uniform and accommodation were provided free, but there was a weekly mess charge for food.

Only about 9,000 records survive out of the 57,000 who served in the WAAC during the First World War. They do not include any for officials (officers), or the several hundred members who died while on active service. Records are surprisingly detailed, including applications to join, references and correspondence about leaving, often to get married. However, there is very little about the member's service, although the casualty form will indicate which units she served with and may give details of periods of leave or time spent in hospital. You may find mention of the Connaught Club, which was the headquarters of the Corps.

These records are online at Findmypast and on The National Archives website. An incomplete nominal roll for members of the Corps is in piece WO 162/16 at Kew, with a list of women drivers employed during the war in WO 162/62. Recommendations for honours and awards are in WO 162/65. The war diaries are only for units that saw service in France and Flanders, but if your ancestor served overseas (and you know the unit) you may well find mention of her arrival or departure, particularly if she was an official.

The eight officials and seventy-five members who died as the result of enemy action can be found in the Soldiers of the Great War database. An extensive collection of material relating to the QMAAC is held in the Templar Study Centre at the National Army Museum in London (www.national-army-musuem.ac.uk), including photographs and personal papers (although there are no nominal rolls or service records).

WRAF

On the establishment of the RAF in April 1918 a separate Women's Royal Air Force (WRAF) was also set up, which was divided into four basic trades: Clerks and Storewomen, Household, Technical and Non-Technical. Initially little training was given, with wages based on existing experience and skills.

The majority of women were employed as clerks, with shorthand typists the most highly paid of all airwomen. Women allocated to the Household section worked the longest hours, doing back-breaking work for the lowest pay. The Technical section covered a wide range of trades, most highly skilled, including tinsmiths, fitters and welders.

Only records for other ranks in the WRAF survive and these are to be found in series AIR 80. No records for officers are known to survive, but those for airwomen are available at Findmypast and on The National

Archives website. They are uninformative, often consisting only of the certificate of discharge on demobilisation, of which each airwoman was given a copy. This gives service number, name, rank, air force trade, date and place of enrolment and date and place of demobilisation. The Library at RAF Museum (www.rafmuseum.org.uk) holds photographs of the WRAF at work, diaries, letters, typed accounts, badges, medals, certificates and other memorabilia.

Further Reading

Mary Ingham, *Tracing Your First World War Service Women Ancestors* (Pen & Sword, 2012) offers an excellent guide to this surprisingly complicated subject.

With the Tanks at Cambrai

Pte John Everest, East Surrey Regiment, saw tanks cause panic among the Germans at Cambrai.

In many accounts of this battle, writers state there was no preliminary bombardment preceding the attack. Although... it was supposed to be a surprise attack, a very intensive bombardment of the enemy positions was kept up for fully half-an-hour. The many batteries of artillery through which we recently had passed, had not been placed there for any aesthetic reasons, as very shortly the enemy would discover, with startling suddenness. Zero hour being 6.30am and having a little time on our hands, we descended into the cellars of some ruined houses overlooking the valley, in which the tanks were being held like so many greyhounds on the leash. As it was very early in a cold November morning, with freezing temperatures, rum ration was distributed to those who wanted it. Needless to say, no soldier refused it.

Before we had time to taste this gift from Jamaica, an ear-splitting detonation rent the air. It was the sharp bark of a naval gun and a signal for all batteries to open fire on the German positions. It was now exactly 6am and the preliminary bombardment so heavy, one had to shout to make

---

conversation possible at all. The great battle of Cambrai and the debut of the tanks in their first big battle formation, was about to be launched upon an astonished world, and still more astonished Germans unlucky enough to oppose us.

The bombardment lasted exactly half-an-hour, and precisely at 6.30am the tanks began to move forward towards the enemy positions. Naturally 'Jerry' had by now got fully aroused by this hellish alarm clock of British guns. No doubt he pinched himself that early November morning to see if it was not some frightful nightmare he was suffering from. What he must have thought when for the first time in his life, he saw scores of huge formidable caterpillar forms crawling towards him, I will leave to the reader's imagination. Although these tanks had not yet learned the art of manoeuvring like the 'waltzing Matildas' of today, yet they were expert at the 'Jitterbug', for as they lounged cumbersomely forward, shaking, heaving, and spitting venomous tongues of flame out of their mouths, they must have given Jerry the Jitters with a vengeance. Moreover the Germans were as defenceless as a child against this frightful apparition of militant animation.

No wonder then the attack was a complete surprise from every viewpoint. This was later verified by prisoners who stated that not a single German soldier had any information that hundreds of tanks were facing them, or that a major offensive was imminent.

It was a truly magnificent sight to watch the tanks advancing, at the same time spitting fire out of their sides, like so many monsters let loose from hell. They gave one the impression of giant caterpillars crawling over the ground, emitting huge tongues of flames, crunching and snorting as their guns belched death and destruction into the German front line trenches, It seemed so unreal and vitally different from our previous experiences in battles, it made one wonder how on earth such ugly monsters could ever be invented, and at the same time crush all obstacles and devour everything in their path. Some seemed to stop dead still and yet at the last moment, spring into life again.

However, not all the tanks reached their objectives, a few seemed to have developed mechanical defects, others were knocked out by direct hits from enemy artillery. The barrage laid down by the German gunners was now devastating, very few square yards of ground escaping without shells blasting holes into it. Through this murderous artillery barrage, we were ordered to advance in the wake of the tanks, first trying to dodge one shell after another in zig-zag fashion.

As I passed the derelict tanks, I began to wonder how many did get through, but in our position the tanks did not have very far to advance and their duty was soon accomplished. We later discovered that the majority of the tanks had triumphed over all obstacles and overawed the enemy to the point of easy surrender. It seemed a miracle as we jumped into the German front line trench no casualties resulted, although most of us were breathless and not a little scared, after escaping that infernal barrage. The Germans overawed by their first sight of the tanks easily surrendered, and as one group advanced with their hands up, a young German soldier, merely a boy, suddenly dropped dead. He had been shot in the back by a Prussian Officer for daring to surrender. Needless to say, this savage act quickly reaped its own reward, for the officer also dropped like a log, shot through the brains. I examined this officer later and verified my previous conviction that the shot had truly found its mark. The treacherous death of the German boy soldier had thus been avenged by one he considered his enemy.

We made a search of dug-outs, but discovered only dead German soldiers in them. The artillery barrage on our positions had now quieted down somewhat, so we quickly got to work reversing the fire steps, and barb wiring the front line. The German front line was now the British front line and although huge twelve-inch shell craters large enough to bury a tank inside them gaped on the fringe, the trench itself was practically intact. It was while reversing the fire steps so that they would face the retreating Germans I began to realise with somewhat of a shock, that we would be on short rations for days to come. The enemy artillery was so heavily bombarding our rear it was impossible for adequate food supplies to reach us in the front line.

J.H. Everest, *The First Battle of the Tanks* (Stockwell, 1942)

Chapter 5

RESEARCHING BATTLES AND UNITS

Structure

During the First World War the British Army expanded from a fairly small organisation in July 1914 to a huge institution by the end of 1918, which historians have suggested was the biggest organisation ever created in Britain. During the War 5.7 million British and Irish men served in the Army at some stage. Or, to put it another way, rather more than 20 per cent of the adult male population wore khaki. The vast majority of these men served overseas. In addition another three million from the Empire (of whom half were Indian) also saw service. They had to be equipped, fed, and trained before being sent into the fighting. It always amazes me that this expansion took place without a major hiccup, and yet so little is known about it today. Recalling his days as a staff officer in 1917, Arthur Behrends wrote:

> …we in France and Flanders in 1917 and 1918 had no complaints about the way in which we were administered. Our medical, transport and supply services had advanced a lot since the days of the Boer and Crimean wars. We were well fed and clothed, when we were wounded or sick we were admirably looked after, leave was given fairly regularly; during my time with the BEF there was no shortage of guns or ammunition, motors, maps or anything. To us it seemed that the vast if at times cumbersome machine worked smoothly, and to us it was the last word in modernity.

The structure of the Army throughout the war remained fairly simple and logical, although the terminology may occasionally confuse, and there are lots of exceptions. The paragraphs below are just a brief overview, and

A very romantic illustration of a charge by the Coldstream Guards during the Battle of the Somme. In fact bayonets were little used by British troops except to toast bread.

more detail is available on the Long Long Trail website. In particular, the army used the word 'corps' in several different ways. Corps lay below army and above division in the Army command structure (see below). The specialist arms, such as the Royal Artillery and Royal Engineers, were also formed into corps. And lastly there was the King's Royal Rifle Corps, an infantry regiment.

The British Expeditionary Force (BEF), as the British Army on the Western Front was known, was divided in December 1914 into a number of armies, each of which was responsible for a specific sector of the front. There were eventually five armies, each of which served in France for all or part of their existence.

Initially command of the BEF was given to Sir John French. In December 1915 he was replaced by Sir Douglas Haig. French and Haig were ultimately under control of the war cabinet in London. Herbert Asquith, who was Prime Minister between August 1914 and December 1916, was generally content to allow the generals to manage the war as they saw fit. This was not a view taken by David Lloyd George when he succeeded Asquith in December 1916. Lloyd George increasingly lost faith in Haig and his generals' ability to win the war without huge numbers of casualties. And his reduction of British forces on the Western Front during the winter of 1917 – in order to reinforce the Italian Front – was a major reason for the success of the German advance in March and April 1918.

Each army was composed of an army HQ, which commanded at least two corps, with various units attached as army troops. In turn the army HQ reported to General Headquarters in St Omer or, from 1916, in the attractive town of Montreuil-Sur-Mer.

Below them the corps replicated, to an extent, the structures of the armies above them. They too had units of army troops attached to their headquarters. And in turn they were responsible for two or more divisions. Twenty-two infantry corps were eventually established, together with separate corps for the cavalry, Australians and New Zealanders (ANZAC), Canadians and Indians.

Army or corps headquarters were generally permanently based in a chateau or similar, fifteen to twenty miles behind the front line. Numbers of headquarters staff were surprisingly small. Both armies and corps were responsible for staff work: planning battles and ensuring that the troops were properly provisioned. The men in the front line had a particular dislike of staff officers, whom they regarded as out of touch with the realities of trench warfare.

Divisions were the highest echelons that were actively engaged in action. They were responsible for implementing the orders sent from corps and army HQs. As a result they were the highest unit an ordinary soldier had affinity with. They were made up of a number of infantry battalions and divisional troops, consisting of units of artillery, engineers, hospitals, and, from 1916, machine-gunners, together with a small headquarters. Very roughly, each division was made up of about 20,000 men from three brigades. The divisions were constantly on the move along the Western Front. In addition, battalions joined and left depending on tactical needs or the shortage of troops.

Below them lay the brigades, which were made up of four battalions, a headquarters and brigade troops. They should not be confused with Royal Artillery brigades, which were equivalent to regiments (and were renamed as such just before the Second World War).

The most important fighting unit was the infantry battalion, which at full strength consisted of about 1,000 men. Battalions were part of a regiment, which through the regimental depot was responsible for recruiting and training men (at least initially) and, through the wives of senior officers, for organising support for men who had been taken prisoner of war and the widows of those who had fallen. Among other duties the depot would also keep the regimental archives and ephemera and publish the regimental magazine.

From 1881 regiments, with the exception of the Rifle Brigade and King's Royal Rifle Corps, were linked to particular counties or cities. The affiliation is often clear from the regimental title, such as the King's Liverpool Regiment or the East Surreys. In peacetime the regiment would recruit from the communities in its local area, but men could choose to join another regiment elsewhere if they wished. Local recruiting continued until the onset of conscription in March 1916, when conscripts began to be assigned to the regiments at random (although volunteers could still choose the regiment they wished to serve with). No conscripts were at the first Battle of the Somme. In addition, units might be broken up and men redrafted to units that had been badly affected by losses in battle. Unit war diaries occasionally record the arrival of new drafts of men, generally with disparaging comments on their quality, but almost never give their names.

In peacetime a regiment was made up of two battalions of regular soldiers, one of which was normally based in Great Britain or Ireland,

Men of the 1st Leicesters inspect a tank which had got stuck in a trench during the Battle of Cambrai, November 1917.

The Pals Battalions

In the early months of the war many new battalions were recruited from groups of local men. On 21 August 1914, the first Pals battalion began to be raised from the stockbrokers of the City of London. In a matter of days 1,600 men had joined what became the 10th Battalion, Royal Fusiliers, unofficially known as the Stockbroker's Battalion. Lord Derby first coined the phrase 'battalion of pals' and recruited enough men to form three battalions of the King's (Liverpool) Regiment in only a week. Battalions such as the Hull Commercials shared an occupation; others, like the Glasgow Tramways Battalion, shared an employer; the Tyneside Irish had a common background. In East Grinstead a sportsman's battalion was raised, including two famous cricketers and the England lightweight boxing champion; London formed a footballers' battalion and units comprised of artists and public schoolboys.

However, these battalions became synonymous with the towns of northern Britain. Men from cities including Manchester, Leeds, Newcastle, Hull, Glasgow and Edinburgh all enlisted in their thousands during the late summer and early autumn of 1914. In Sheffield doors opened on 10 September and the new battalion (the 12th Battalion, York and Lancaster Regiment, nicknamed the Sheffield City Battalion) reached full strength in only two days, encouraged by the optimistic placards reading 'To Berlin – via Corn Exchange' where recruitment was taking place. The battalion's historian Richard Sparling later wrote that there were: '£500 a year business men, stockbrokers, engineers, chemists, metallurgical experts, University and public school men, medical students, journalists, schoolmasters, craftsmen, shop assistants, secretaries, and all sorts of clerks.' Among their number was miner and poet John William Streets, who came from Whitwell on the edge of the Peak District.

The most famous of these units was the 11th Battalion, East Lancashire Regiment, members of which largely came from the small Lancashire cotton town of Accrington and surrounding areas.

After initial training in Britain (the Sheffield Pals began by drilling at Bramall Lane football ground), the first Pals battalions began to arrive on the Western Front from mid-1915. The Stockbrokers was one of the first, landing at Boulogne on 30 July 1915, although it took until late February 1916 for the Accrington Pals to cross the Channel.

Most Pals battalions were not to see their first major action until the first day of the Battle of the Somme on 1 July 1916. Previously they had been engaged in training in preparation for the 'big push', with short periods of time in the front line. During the battle many units sustained heavy casualties, which had a significant impact on their communities. The 11th East Lancashires were all but destroyed on 1 July 1916; of the 720 Accrington Pals who took part in the attack 584 were killed, wounded or missing. Almost every household in the town was affected in some way.

With the introduction of conscription in 1916, the close-knit nature of the Pals battalions could never be replicated. Men were now assigned to whichever unit needed them.

Further Reading

Pen & Sword have published histories of most Pals battalions. Andrew Martin has captured the atmosphere of a Pals Battalion in his novel *The Somme Stations* (Faber, 2012).

There are also a number of websites devoted to Pals Battalions. In particular there are several websites devoted to the Accrington Pals, including the excellent www.pals.org.uk.

while the other was overseas, generally in India. The third and fourth battalions were territorial units made up of part-time soldiers. On the outbreak of war in 1914 there was a huge expansion of the Army as men flocked to the colours. New infantry battalions were created almost on a daily basis. Some Territorial battalions were split to form cadres for new units. In some regiments these were simply sequentially numbered (typically sixth and seventh), but in others they were given a number that showed their ancestry. For example, if the 5th King's Own Yorkshire Light Infantry was split, the two resulting battalions were numbered 1/5th and 2/5th. Other battalions raised for the war were known as service battalions. These took their numbers immediately after the original Territorial battalions. The Hampshire Regiment, for example, eventually had nineteen battalions.

An infantry battalion was made up of a battalion headquarters and four companies. The battalion was usually commanded by a lieutenant colonel, with a major as second in command. In addition, at battalion HQ there would be an adjutant, a junior officer who was in charge of battalion administration including preparing the war diary; a quartermaster responsible for stores and transport; and a medical officer, who was on detachment from the RAMC.

Here you would also find the regimental sergeant major (or RSM, the most senior non-commissioned officer) plus a number of specialist roles filled by sergeants, including quartermasters, cooks, signallers and the orderly room clerk. There were also a number of specialist sections, such as the signallers (who were often men being groomed as potential officers), machine-gunners (although in January 1916 they were transferred to the new Machine Gun Corps), drivers for the horse-drawn transport and stretcher-bearers, who traditionally were the musicians of the battalion band.

The four battalion companies were generally given letters A–D. Each company was commanded by a major or captain. There was also a company sergeant major (CSM) and the 'quarterbloke', the company quartermaster sergeant (CQMS).

Companies were divided into four platoons, under lieutenants and second lieutenants, sometimes referred to as subalterns. Each platoon consisted of four sections. Generally each section comprised twelve men under an NCO. These were the men that an ordinary soldier would work with, fight with and socialise with. A private might also have dealings with the platoon commander, and perhaps know the company and battalion commanders by sight.

In some ways the organisation of the battalion was similar to that of a secondary school. If you think back to your time at school, you would know the form teacher and others who taught you, but might know only by sight the head teacher and heads of subjects. And the chances are that you would spend most of your day with a small group of friends who were in the same class as you.

Although most men serving in France were assigned to infantry units, by the end of the war the proportion of men at 'the sharp end', in Winston

The Unit War Diary for 21st Northumberland Fusiliers (Tyneside Scottish) for 1 July 1916. It briefly describes the traumatic events of the day. (*TNA WO 95/2462*)

Churchill's memorable phrase, was declining fast. There were a number of specialist services or arms, such as the Royal Flying Corps, Royal Artillery, Royal Engineers and Royal Army Medical Corps, whose numbers grew as the War became increasingly industrial in nature. Fortunately, the records for these arms are much the same as for the infantry, although it is almost impossible to identify which particular unit a gunner, sapper, driver or stretcher-bearer served with.

In particular the British Army was becoming much more mechanised. Even if the tactics and uniforms had changed, the British Expeditionary Force of 1914 would have been clearly recognisable to the men who fought at Waterloo a century earlier. But by 1918 the Army was a very different institution. The most obvious example of the mechanisation of the British Army was the tank. These land ships, or land crabs, as they were initially called, were first used on 15 September 1916, when thirty-six tanks made an *en masse* attack at Flers. Originally there had been fifty machines, but these thirty-ton beasts could not cope with the harsh lunar landscape of the churned-up ground and fourteen broke down or got bogged down in the mud. The sudden appearance of the tanks stunned the Germans, but the machines were initially notoriously unreliable, largely because they were introduced before their mechanical faults had been ironed out.

Tanks were first used with real success at the Battle of Cambrai in October 1917, when nearly 500 tanks helped drive a twelve-mile breach through the German front line. Unfortunately the infantry were unable to capitalise on this, so British gains were minimal. Tanks really came into their own during the advances of 'the Hundred Days' between August and November 1918, spearheading attacks on German lines supported by the infantry. By the end of the war nearly 2,500 tanks had been built. Originally tanks came under the responsibilities of the Machine Gun Corps, but a separate Tank Corps was established in July 1917.

The most important of the specialist arms was the Royal Artillery. Artillery, and its use, was key to the eventual Allied victory. The military historian John Terraine, in his 1982 book *White Heat – the new warfare 1914–18*, argues: 'The war of 1914–18 was an artillery war: artillery was the battle-winner, artillery was what caused the greatest loss of life, the most dreadful wounds, and the deepest fear.' The British Expeditionary Force crossed the Channel in August 1914 with twenty-four five-inch guns. By the Armistice Sir Douglas Haig had 6,500 field pieces, ranging in size from three to eighteen inches in calibre. In addition there were mobile gun platforms – tanks – and thousands of aircraft to help direct artillery barrage or direct bomb enemy targets.

Initially, in preparation for big battles the British used their artillery in massive barrages for days on end, with the intention of destroying the German defences. On the day itself troops would advance behind a wall of artillery fire – a moving barrage – which would knock out any remaining enemy positions. This was the theory. In practice, although the preparatory barrages were terrible, the Germans were generally well dug-in and thus had very effective notice of a forthcoming British attack. Because there was almost no communication between the advancing troops and the artillery providing the moving barrage support, it was all too easy for artillery to shell the advancing troops or fail to destroy machine-gun nests and the like. New tactics of shorter, more concentrated bursts, with the aim of providing greater support of the advancing troops

Howitzers in action during the Battle of Arras. During the last two years of the war the increasing mechanisation of the war, as well as its horrors, were increasingly captured by teams of photographers.

were introduced, initially rather tentatively, at the Battle of Ancre in November 1916, but progressively along the whole of the Western Front during 1918.

The Germans also effectively used their artillery to destroy British positions and make life difficult for men in the front line and those coming to relieve them. At about dusk the Germans would often launch a fifteen-minute barrage, known to the British as the 'Hate'. In turn this might lead to an Allied response.

The Royal Regiment of Artillery comprised three elements. The Royal Horse Artillery was armed with light, mobile, horse-drawn guns that in theory provided firepower in support of the cavalry. However, in the immobile conditions of the Western Front it was increasingly supplemented by the Royal Field Artillery. The Royal Field Artillery was the largest arm of the artillery and it was responsible for the medium-calibre guns and howitzers deployed close to the front line. Finally, there was the Royal Garrison Artillery, developed from fortress-based artillery located on British coasts. It was armed with heavy, large-calibre guns and howitzers with immense destructive power. Royal Artillery units, usually called brigades, were responsible to brigade, divisional and corps Commanders Royal Artillery (CRAs).

Less well known are the Royal Engineers, who had many different specialisms, including transportation (such as building and maintaining the maze of narrow gauge railways that carried supplies up to the front), tunnelling under enemy lines and laying and exploding mines, surveying and preparing trench maps, chemical warfare, designing and preparing camouflage and even running the postal service. This last was undoubtedly the most appreciated by the men at the front!

Despite the arrival of the lorry, the tank and the aeroplane, the First World War was not a heavily mechanised war. There was a constant demand for labour, to move stores and ammunition, mend roads and build dug-outs, and this is what the infantryman did when he was not in the front line.

For more details see the relevant pages on the Long Long Trail and Western Front Association websites (which the paragraphs above are based on).

Published Sources

Orders of Battle

Orders of battle (often referred to as Orbats) offer a guide to the British Army based on its structure. They can be of value because they list under which division, corps or army a battalion or unit served and when they moved between the higher echelons. What you won't find, however, is the physical location of individual units. Orders are explained in more detail at www.greatwar.co.uk/research/military-records/ww1-orders-of-battle.htm. The Long Long Trail website contains many orders of battle arranged by echelon or by unit.

Also of use are Ray Westlake's *British Battalions On The Western Front* (Pen & Sword, 2000) for the period between January and June 1915, *British Battalions In France And Belgium 1914* (Pen & Sword, 1997) and *Tracing British Battalions on the Somme* (Pen & Sword, 2009).

A useful shortcut is to look at the description of the battalion or unit war diary to be found in the piece description on the Discovery Catalogue on The National Archives website, which will give you the brigade and division that the battalion or unit was serving with for at least part of its existence.

Official Histories

During the 1920s the government commissioned teams of historians, under Brigadier General James Edmonds, to prepare detailed official histories of the war, formally known as the *History of the Great War based on Official Documents*. The intention was to learn lessons, both tactical and logistic, from the war and also to provide an authoritative historical account. Historians have often dismissed them as being mere propaganda: 'official but not history' in military writer Basil Liddell Hart's tart phrase. They are nonetheless worth consulting, if for no other reason than that they contain a superb series of maps of the battlefields. However, they are likely to be hard going for the novice, as they can be quite technical.

There are separate multi-volume series for each year on the Western Front, which are listed on the Long Long Trail website www.1914-1918.net/official.html and the Great War website www.greatwar.co.uk/research/books/ww1-official-history.htm. Many reference libraries have incomplete sets. Both the IWM and the Naval and Military Press have reprinted many volumes.

Before the histories were published drafts were sent to officers who had fought in the campaign for their comments. Their replies can be very informative and offer honest insights into how battles were viewed by officers, although their responses often contain more than a hint of hindsight. Occasionally they offer insights into how battle was fought by the troops on the ground. Robert Greig, who commanded the 101st Brigade on 1 July 1916, wrote to Brigadier Edmonds:

> The removal of the wounded after the morning of July 1st was impossible until that night. The stretcher bearers were quite inadequate in number and by 3am were completely exhausted. At that time the dug-outs in our first line trenches and in some of the German first line trenches were full of wounded. The whole of No Man's Land on the 34th Divisional front was covered with dead and wounded. On the night of the 2nd July, great efforts were made to remove these men from No Man's Land and the German front line. Additional fatigue parties of stretcher bearers in groups under officers were supplied by the Corps, and by the night of 3rd July, most of the men still alive on the Divisional

front had been brought in. A few days later we buried 2,200 men on the Divisional front. Except on that occasion the removal of the wounded was carried out very well. The breakdown of July 1st was due to the exceptional numbers, which were too great for the ordinary organisation to deal with.

Greig also described the work of Colonel Rose, a water diviner, in finding water on the battlefield: 'At the places he indicated wells were dug or borings made, pumps erected and quantities of water were obtained...' (Letter of 22 July 1930, TNA CAB 45/134.)

The correspondence, together with a small collection of private diaries and related paperwork, including several enemy accounts, is at The National Archives in series CAB 45/215-261.

Regimental Histories

Any regiment worth its name will have had several histories written about it. The first were published in the mid-nineteenth century and they are still being written today. Most regiments and service corps have specific histories relating to the unit during the First World War and between the wars. Inevitably they vary greatly in quality and interest. The best include interviews with former officers or copies of letters they wrote home describing incidents and battles, but most offer a workmanlike overview of what each battalion did, theatre by theatre, month by month. Although they are now rather dated, serious researchers should not ignore them. In particular they remain a key source for regimental museums and archives. Also worth looking out for are the divisional histories, which describe the war from the perspective of the division HQ.

There is a detailed bibliography arranged by regiment and arm provided by the Army Museums Ogilby Trust (www.armymuseums. org.uk). More complete are probably Roger Perkins, *Regiments: Regiments and Corps of the British Empire and Commonwealth 1758–1993: a Critical Bibliography of their Published Histories* (David and Charles, 1994) and Arthur S. White, *A Bibliography of Regimental Histories of the British Army* (London, Stamp Exchange, 1988).

The Imperial War Museum and National Army Museum have major collections. In addition The National Archives and the Society of

Genealogists libraries also have good sets. Regimental museums and local libraries should have those for units raised in their area. The Military and Naval Press have republished many volumes in recent years.

Since the 1970s there has been an explosion of unofficial battalion histories, such as the series about the Pals battalions for Pen & Sword, which describes the activities of individual units. Most are meticulously researched and illustrated and are well worth looking out for.

Regimental Magazines

By the 1920s almost every regiment published a quarterly magazine, which contained many stories about regimental activities and listed promotions, the awards of education certificates, cups for marksmanship and the minutiae of everyday life in the Army, which on the whole was not recorded elsewhere. You might well find obituaries of old soldiers and memoirs of particular battles or actions experienced by the writer.

There is no national collection of these magazines, although the National Army Museum and, to a lesser degree, the Imperial War Museum have incomplete sets. The best place to look is in regimental archives. The Royal Logistics Corps has published online those for its 'forming corps', notably the Army Service Corps and Army Ordnance Corps. Details at www.rlcarchive.org. Miles Templer (www.templer.net) has published a small selection on CD.

Official Despatches

After each war or campaign commanders-in-chief are expected to summarise the successes and failures in a despatch that is then published in the *London Gazette*. Those for the First World War are surprisingly readable. In his final despatch, published in 1919, Haig used the services of the writer John Buchan. In it they traditionally mention service personnel of all ranks worthy of special praise, hence the term Mention in Despatches (sometimes abbreviated to MID).

The reports are now rarely used by historians, but might prove of interest if your ancestor was one of the 103,000 men and women who were Mentioned in Despatches. It is rare, however, to find out why an individual was so commemorated.

The despatches are available online through the *London Gazette* (www.thegazette.co.uk) and republished by Martin Mace and John Grehan in *Despatches from the Front: the Western Front 1914–1916* (Pen & Sword, 2013). The texts are also available on the Long Long Trail website, although Chris Baker does not include any of the lists of names which accompanied the originals.

Researching Actions

Unit War Diaries

War diaries are the most important source for researching activities by Army units, whether they were in the front line or stationed a long way from the action. They were introduced in 1908 and are still kept by units in action today.

The diaries were designed to record unit activities, particularly when it was in action. This, it was felt, would help analysis by historians and strategists so that they could learn lessons for future wars: they are very much the first draft of history. They were kept by infantry battalions and artillery batteries as well as by higher echelons, such as brigades, divisions and even armies, as well as by more specialist units such as mobile hospitals, signals companies and field bakeries. During the First World War, with very few exceptions, they only survive for units that served outside Britain and Ireland.

For researchers they are the raw material of history because they contain the immediate records of each day's activities, generally unfiltered by further reflection, and they occasionally contain the thoughts and feelings of the men compiling them. The Unit War Diary for the 11th East Lancashire Regiment (the Accrington Pals) for 1 July 1916 reads:

> The battalion was ordered to go forward in 4 waves accompanied by details from the 94th Machine Gun Company and the 12th Battn. K.O.Y.L.I. (Pioneers), the hour for attack being 7.30 a.m.
>
> When the infantry advanced, heavy rifle and machine gun fire was opened from in front and enfilade from the direction of the POINT and GOMMECOURT WOOD. A heavy artillery barrage was also placed on our front line trenches. From information

brought back by wounded it appears that only a few reached the enemy front line and were able to enter their trenches owing to the intensity of the Machine Gun and rifle fire. Small parties penetrated as far as the German fourth line, but were not heard of again. During the day the unwounded men who returned were utilised to occupy our front line trenches. (TNA WO 95/2366)

Naturally war diaries are only concerned with the occurrences in one specific unit. To get the best from them you need to use them in conjunction with other records, such as published histories, memoirs and diaries, and official histories. It is a shame that they have not been more used by popular historians, but perhaps this will change once they are all online.

War diaries were generally completed either by the commanding officer or, in larger units, by the adjutant, the junior officer who was responsible for the general administration of the unit. Inevitably war diaries reflect the enthusiasm that the officer compiling the war diary had for the task, but most are reasonably detailed particularly when the unit was in the front line.

It is very unusual to find individual privates and non-commissioned officers mentioned unless they had received an immediate gallantry award, and even then they might not be included. However, officers were generally named, particularly when they were killed, wounded or awarded gallantry medals, or were sent out to lead a patrol into No Man's Land, returned from leave or left on a training course.

As well as the diaries themselves there may be accompanying appendices. These might consist of regimental orders, plans of attack, maps and other ephemeral information, including on occasion lists of officers and men awarded gallantry medals. Of particular interest are typewritten operational reports, which supplement entries in the war diaries themselves.

It is important to remember that diaries were compiled at battalion headquarters. Companies or sections might actually be based some distance from headquarters, and their experiences could be very different, yet this may not be recorded. To an extent this is excusable in the heat and chaos of battle.

Curiously, it is often difficult to know exactly where a battalion or unit was based. You may need a decent map of the area to be able to pick up the village where they were stationed behind the line. A fairly large-scale road atlas of France might be sufficient. If a map reference is given then you should be able to find it on the appropriate trench map (see below).

War Diaries: Higher Echelons

War diaries exist for brigades, divisions and higher echelons. Inevitably there is less about day-to-day activities on the front, but more about planning battles and trench raids and meeting the logistical demands of tens of thousands of men. However, I have often found copies of operational reports among them that are no longer with the battalion records. Certainly it is worth checking the brigade diaries as well as the battalion ones, as these can give an overview of what was actually going in the trenches that a battalion war diary cannot. In particular you may find recommendations for the award of gallantry medals, as these had to be approved by the officer commanding the brigade.

At the highest echelons the term war diary is rather a misnomer. The actual war diary is often no more than a page or two per month, and may just record the visits of senior officers and other inconsequential matters. The real meat lies in the accompanying appendices, which can include orders, reports, plans, maps and occasionally photographs. There will be much material about planning and preparation for battle, which questions the myth that the men in the front line were not equipped for trench warfare. The appendices are doubly important because so much about how the war was planned or organised was destroyed in the disastrous fire of September 1940.

There should be war diaries for each component part of divisions, corps and armies, that is, general staff (responsible for the planning for and direction of the fighting) adjutant and quartermaster general (administration and supplying troops in the field), artillery, engineers, and medical, as well as those infantry and cavalry units which were attached to headquarters.

War Diaries: Location and Use

An almost complete set of diaries is at The National Archives in series WO 95 (with a few 'confidential war diaries' in WO 154, which generally mention individuals who appeared before courts martial). They are arranged by army, corps, division and brigade, although in practice this doesn't matter because it is easy to pick up individual units through the Discovery catalogue. The diaries are arranged by month and consist of entries in pencil on loose sheets of paper. Appendices tend to be typed or in the form of cyclostyle copies.

TNA has digitised the diaries for units that served in France and Flanders only. It costs £3.30 to download a war diary, although, at the time of writing, you can still visit Kew to read the originals. This is amazing value for money, but there is one major disadvantage. Unless you have superfast broadband it can take hours to download diaries, because the individual files are generally massive.

Fortunately, there is an alternative in the form of the Naval and Military Archive. Instead of downloading the whole diary you can read war diaries page by page, which is fine if you want to find out about a particular 'stunt' or see whether there is anything about an individual casualty. The quality of the images is top notch, although the site itself is not terribly user-friendly. This is a subscription site. Ancestry also has sets of war diaries, although they are so badly indexed as to be almost worthless.

Despite all the evidence to the contrary TNA does not have a complete set of diaries, so if the unit diary appears to be missing it is worth approaching the regimental archives as they often have duplicate copies. This is particularly the case with the Royal Artillery as TNA's holdings are rather patchy.

A few regimental museums have transcribed their sets of war diaries and put them online, generally free of charge. For example, the Wardrobe Museum in Salisbury, which is the regimental museum for the Berkshire and Wiltshire regiments, has put up the battalion war diaries for both world wars (www.thewardrobe.org.uk).

Further Reading

All the war diaries for units that took part in the events of 1 July 1916 have been transcribed by John Grehan and Martin Mace and published in *Slaughter on the Somme* (Pen & Sword, 2013).

Other Reports

Although much has long since been destroyed, it is still possible to work out how the Battle of the Somme was planned and how the battle was perceived by headquarters as it happened. There is a lot of material in appendices of higher echelon war diaries. In addition there are reports and files for all aspects of the war on the Western Front in Military Headquarters: Correspondence and Papers (series WO 158).

One of the major problems facing headquarters was the lack of information coming back from the troops on the ground. Neither the staff, nor the supporting artillery, had any real idea where British troops were as they advanced into German lines. Communications with front line troops were erratic at best. This comes out clearly in the 4th Army Summary of Operations (WO 158/322-326) for the period between 1 July and 12 November 1916. The Army was largely reliant on reports from RFC pilots. At 11.08am on 1 July, for example, headquarters received a report that read:

> Two white flares seen south of La Boisselle, one north west of Orvillers. One or two infantry on Sandy Patch 300 yards south of La Boisselle. North of the Bapaume road is very quiet and hardly any shelling. There is a great deal of shelling between Fricourt and Mametz, smoke so thick that nothing can be seen.

At 2.45pm the report read:

> 29th Division are all back in their own front line trenches except for the two battalions who pushed onto Station Road. There are a few men holding Hawthorn Crater. They were unable to make the projected attack at 12.30pm owing to the congestion of wounded etc in our front line and communication trenches.

At 8.50pm the Army HQ desperately telegraphed divisions:

> Could you give us any indication from reports of wounded or
> otherwise of extent of enemy casualties today. Brief reply on
> telephone will suffice. (TNA WO 158/322)

Also of use are the private diaries of Sir Douglas Haig, and the commander
of Fourth Army, Sir Henry Rawlinson. The National Archives has copies
of Haig's diaries in series WO 256, although it may be easier to use Gary
Sheffield and John Bourne, *Douglas Haig: War Diaries and Letters 1914–1918*
(Weidenfeld & Nicolson, 2005). Rawlinson's diaries remain unpublished
and are at the Churchill Archives Centre in Cambridge.

Photographs and Film

The largest collection by far of First World War related material is at the
Imperial War Museum. At the heart of the museum's collections are
40,000 official photographs showing all aspects of the war. As it took time
for a satisfactory system to be set up, and particularly to overcome
suspicion from the military authorities, the photographic record is more
comprehensive from mid-1916 onwards than for the first half of the war.
Initially a number of soldiers took cameras with them to the battlefields,
but they were banned in the spring of 1915.

This collection is supplemented by material donated by individual
servicemen. Many images, but certainly not all, are described in the online
catalogue at www.iwm.org.uk/collections/search.

Regimental Museums and local studies libraries should also have
collections of material. The Honourable Artillery Company archive, for
example, has many photographs of soldiers who fell during the war,
because the company's secretary of the day wrote to the deceased's
families asking for pictures.

The Imperial War Museum's Film and Video Archive also has by far the
largest collection of films. Its collection is described in Roger Smithers (ed),
The Imperial War Museum Film Catalogue Volume 1: The First World War
(Flick Books, 1997).

If you are researching the Somme campaign then you really should
watch the film *The Battle of the Somme* and the sequel *The Battle of Ancre*, as

they offer a unique picture of the British Army on the Western Front. The film, thought one soldier: 'did not give you much idea of a bombardment, but casual scenes in and on the way to the trenches are well chosen and amazingly like what happens.' This ground-breaking film was seen by two-thirds of the British population on its release in late 1916. It is now available on YouTube, or on DVD. However, do not expect a modern film. The film is jerky, editing is pretty minimal, with long tracking shots of men marching or moving munitions, and there are very few action shots of the battle itself. YouTube also has a German film *Bei unseren Helden an der Somme* (Heroes on the Somme) with a suitably bombastic military band accompaniment.

Also worth checking out are newsreels – short news stories shown at local cinemas. Those for the First World War largely concentrate on the 'home front'. There is a list at http://bufvc.ac.uk/newsonscreen/search. British Pathé (www.britishpathe.com) and Movietone (www.movietone.com) have clips from the newsreels they made available on their websites free of charge.

It is also well worth visiting YouTube as many films, including short documentaries and original films, have been posted there. Of particular interest is the 1976 BBC documentary marking the 60th anniversary of the Battle of the Somme, which includes interviews with many veterans, and the Richard Holmes 1996 War Walks programme on walking the Somme. Bizarrely there is also a re-creation of the 'First Day' using Lego pieces, which is surprisingly effective.

Trench Maps

From early 1915 British surveyors and mapmakers began to map the trenches using sketches drawn by observers in aircraft perilously flying along the Western Front.

The trenches were originally mapped at a scale of 1:10,000, that is roughly six inches to the mile, with red lines (for German trenches) and blue (for British). The colours were reversed in 1918. The maps are superimposed on a ghostly backdrop of the villages, woods and railways found on pre-war maps of Flanders and France, upon which these maps were based. Ammunition dumps, hospitals and other facilities reveal how far the countryside for miles behind the front line was appropriated by the military. Close to the front line the maps show the intricacies of the

Trenches in the Newfoundland Memorial Park at Beaumont-Hamel. (*Author*)

trench systems, indicating individual command posts, machine-guns, field batteries and so on, all plotted from air photographs.

The maps are very detailed, although it has to be said that they can be difficult to use. They will be of most use to people who already have a knowledge of the terrain.

Major collections of maps are held by both The National Archives (series WO 153 and WO 297) and the Imperial War Museum. Local regimental museums and other archives may also have smaller collections.

Many maps, but certainly not all, have been scanned by McMaster University in Canada and can be viewed at http://library.mcmaster.ca/maps/ww1/ndx5to40.htm.

You can buy facsimiles in several formats. Paper copies of selected maps have been published by G.H. Smith and Son (www.ghsmithbookshop. com). Otherwise sets are available on CD. The best such collection is undoubtedly *The National Archives British Trench Map Atlas* from Naval and Military Press (www.great-war-trench-maps.com/watm.htm) with hundreds of different maps in various editions. The Western Front Association has also published a small collection for the major battle zones. Great War Digital (www.greatwardigital.com) is a company selling digitised trench maps that can be used in GPS systems. They are probably of greatest use when touring the battlefields.

Further Reading

The best introduction to trench maps and how to use them is at www.greatwar.co.uk/research/maps/british-army-ww1-trench-maps.htm. In particular there is a useful guide to interpreting map references that you might find in a war diary. Also useful is Chris Baker's explanation at www.1914-1918.net/trench_maps.htm. The best book is Peter Chasseaud, *Topography of Armageddon: a British trench map atlas of the Western Front, 1914–1918* (Mapbooks, 1991). Also of interest is Peter Chasseaud, *Artillery's Astrologers – A History of British Field Survey and Mapping on the Western Front, 1914–1918* (Mapbooks, 1999); and *Mapping the First World War: The Great War through maps from 1914–1918* (Imperial War Museum, 2013).

The Attack

Pte Richard Tawney of the Manchester Regiment was another soldier in the first wave of the attack on the German lines on 1 July 1916.

It was a glorious morning, and, as though there were some mysterious sympathy between the wonders of the ear and of the eye, the bewildering tumult seemed to grow more insistent with the growing brilliance of the atmosphere and the intenser blue of the July sky. The sound was different, not only in magnitude, but in quality, from anything known to me. It was not a succession of explosions or a continuous roar; I, at least, never heard either a gun or a bursting shell. It was not a noise; it was a symphony. It did not move; it hung over us. It was as though the air were full of a vast and agonized passion, bursting now into groans and sighs, now into shrill screams and pitiful whimpers, shuddering beneath terrible blows, torn by unearthly whips, vibrating with the solemn pulse of enormous wings. And the supernatural tumult did not pass in this direction or that. It did not begin, intensify, decline, and end. It was poised in the air, a stationary panorama of sound, a condition of the atmosphere, not the creation of man. It seemed that one had only to lift one's eyes to be appalled by the writhing of the tormented element above one, that a hand raised ever so little above the level of the trench would be sucked away into a whirlpool revolving with cruel and incredible velocity over infinite depths. And this feeling, while it filled one with awe, filled one also with triumphant exultation, the exultation of struggling against a storm in mountains, or watching the irresistible course of a swift and destructive river. Yet at the same time one was intent on practical details, wiping the trench dirt off the bolt of one's rifle, reminding the men of what each was to do, and when the message went round, 'five minutes to go,' seeing that all bayonets were fixed. My captain, a brave man and a good officer, came along and borrowed a spare watch off me. It was the last time I saw him.

At 7.30 we went up the ladders, doubled through the gaps in the wire, and lay down, waiting for the line to form up on each side of us. When it was ready we went forward, not doubling, but at a walk. For we had nine hundred yards of rough ground to the trench which was our first objective, and about fifteen hundred to a further trench where we were to wait for orders. There was a bright light in the air, and the tufts of coarse grass were grey with dew.

I hadn't gone ten yards before I felt a load fall from me. There's a sentence at the end of *The Pilgrim's Progress* which has always struck me as one of the most awful things imagined by man: 'Then I saw that there was a way to Hell, even from the Gates of Heaven, as well as from the City of Destruction.' To have gone so far and be rejected at last! Yet undoubtedly man walks between precipices, and no one knows the rottenness in him till he cracks, and then it's too late. I had been worried by the thought: 'Suppose one should lose one's head and get other men cut up! Suppose one's legs should take fright and refuse to move!' Now I knew it was all right. I shouldn't be frightened and I shouldn't lose my head. Imagine the joy of that discovery! I felt quite happy and self-possessed. It wasn't courage. That, I imagine, is the quality of facing danger which one knows to be danger, of making one's spirit triumph over the bestial desire to live in this body.

But I knew that I was in no danger. I knew I shouldn't be hurt; knew it positively, much more positively than I know most things I'm paid for knowing. I understood in a small way what Saint-Just meant when he told the soldiers who protested at his rashness that no bullet could touch the emissary of the Republic. And all the time, in spite of one's inner happiness, one was shouting the sort of thing that NCO's do shout and no one attends to: 'Keep your extension'; 'Don't bunch'; 'Keep up on the left'. I remember being cursed by an orderly for yelling the same things days after in the field-hospital.

Well, we crossed three lines that had once been trenches, and tumbled into the fourth, our first objective. 'If it's all like this, it's a cake-walk,' said a little man beside me, the kindest and bravest of friends, whom no weariness could discourage or danger daunt, a brick-layer by trade, but one who could turn his hand to anything, the man whom of all others I would choose to have beside me at a pinch; but he's dead. While the men dug furiously to make a fire-step, I looked about me. On the parados lay a wounded man of another battalion, shot, to judge by the blood on his tunic, through the loins or stomach. I went to him, and he grunted, as if to say, 'I am in terrible pain; you must do something for me; you must do something for me; you must do something for me.' I hate touching wounded men – moral cowardice, I suppose. One hurts them so much and there's so little to be done. I tried, without much success, to ease his equipment, and then thought of getting him into the trench. But it was crowded with men and there was no place to put him. So I left him. He grunted again angrily, and looked at me with hatred as well as pain in his eyes. It was horrible. It was a though he cursed me for being alive and strong when he was in torture. I tried to forget him by snatching a spade from one of the men and working on the parapet. But one's mind wasn't in it; it was over 'there', there where 'they' were waiting for us...

Anyway, when we'd topped a little fold in the ground, we walked straight into a zone of machine-gun fire. The whole line dropped like one man, some dead and wounded, the rest taking instinctively to such cover as the ground offered. On my immediate right three men lay in a shell-hole. With their heads and feet just showing, they looked like fish in a basket.

Taken from R.H. Tawney, *The Attack and Other Papers* (New York, 1952). The piece was originally written for the *Westminster Gazette* for publication in August 1916.

Chapter 6

THE WAR IN THE AIR

The First World War saw a rapid expansion in the air services and the work undertaken by aircraft. At the Battle of Loos in September 1915 the Royal Flying Corps (RFC) had twelve squadrons, each with eighteen aircraft on strength. The number had more than doubled to twenty-seven squadrons by the following July. The RFC devoted its time to supporting the Army on the Western Front and elsewhere by initially operating reconnaissance missions, and later through artillery spotting and bombing German targets in France and Belgium. There was a secondary but equally important aim of maintaining dominance of the air, ensuring that German planes could not operate over British lines.

Until February 1916 the Royal Naval Air Service (RNAS) was responsible for the air defence of Britain (when it was transferred to the RFC), and was the pioneer of strategic bombing against Germany and sites in occupied France from its base in Dunkirk. In addition the service operated patrols from coastal air stations in Britain and from ships.

The Royal Air Force was formed on 1 April 1918 as a marriage of the Royal Flying Corps (RFC) and the Royal Naval Air Service (RNAS).

The mobility and freedom of the air was often contrasted with the stalemate of the trenches. Even so the lives of pilots and observers were usually merry and generally short. During the five months of the Battle of the Somme the Royal Flying Corps lost 782 aircraft and 576 pilots. In 1917 the life expectancy of a pilot on the Western Front was between eleven days and three weeks. That is if they survived the brutal period of training. Of the 14,000 pilots and aircrew in the RFC who were killed, well over half lost their lives during training. An informative database containing details of men who served as pilots, observers and gunners is at www.airhistory.org.uk/rfc/people_index.html.

A unique resource is the magazine *Flight*, which has been published since 1909 and is now available online in a fully searchable form at www.flightglobal.com/pdfarchive. It contains much about the men, the machines and the activities of the British air services during the First World War.

Service Records

Records for RAF and predecessor services are now largely online. Unfortunately they are more informative about pilots and observers (the men who in the Second World War would become known as aircrew) than the men who maintained the machines or ran squadrons and other units on a day-to-day basis (groundcrew). Indexes to squadron nominal rolls (mainly listing aircrew) are available on the excellent Air History website www.airhistory.org.uk/rfc/people_index.html.

For men who served before the creation of the RAF in April 1918 you should also check the sources for the Army (RFC) and the Navy (RNAS).

There are Medal Index Cards for nearly 27,000 officers and airmen who transferred from the RFC to the RAF in April 1918. Where there is no card, exactly the same information can be found on the service records of airmen (but not on officers' records).

The *London Gazette* (thegazette.co.uk) records the promotion of RAF officers and, to a degree, lists postings, as well as the award of gallantry medals.

Officers

The National Archives has service records for RAF officers and airmen who were discharged before the early 1920s. They include details about next of kin, civilian occupation, units in which an individual served, appointments and promotions, and honours and medals awarded. In addition comments may have been added by training officers about the individuals' flying skills or (more likely) lack of them. The records are considerably more informative for pilots, navigators, and observers than for the engineering staff or the administrators. The records are all online via the TNA website and Findmypast.

For pilots it is worth looking at the Royal Aero Club Aviators' Certificates on Ancestry, which contains approximately 28,000 index cards and thirty-four photograph albums of aviators who were issued with their flying licences by the Royal Aero Club, mainly between 1910 and late 1915. Many of these pilots would have been in the skies above Loos and the Somme. The cards include name, birth date, birthplace, nationality, rank or profession, date and place of certificate, and certificate number.

RNAS officers' records are in ADM 273. They are arranged by service number order, although there is an index available through Discovery. The records will give you details of which units he served with, next-of-kin and comments by superior offices about performance and conduct.

Information about the officers and ratings of the RNAS who died during the war are in series ADM 242 (and online through Findmypast).

On the formation of the RAF a new *Air Force List* was published on the lines of the Army and Navy Lists with brief details of officers. These are available at https://archive.org. The one for April 1918 is also online at www.rafmuseumstoryvault.org.uk.

The war service of many pilots, particularly those regarded as 'aces' (that is those who shot down five or more enemy aircraft), have been researched and published in books, such as C.F. Shores, N.L.R. Franks and R. Guest, *Above the Trenches. A Complete Record of the Fighter Aces and Units of the British Empire Air Forces, 1915–1920* (1990, with a supplement in 2002) and for bomber crews their *Above the War Fronts: A Complete Record of the British Two-Seater Bomber Pilot and Observer Aces* (1997).

Other Ranks

Records of RAF other ranks are online through Findmypast. Apart from personal details, these records include dates of enlistment and discharge, promotions and units served with, brief notes of medical and disciplinary history, and dates of service overseas. In addition they contain the same information as the Medal Index Cards, so if there isn't an actual card for your man, this is a more than adequate alternative.

TNA has a muster roll of all other ranks who joined the new RAF in April 1918, showing their ranks and trades. This is also available on Findmypast and, free of charge, at www.rafmuseumstoryvault.org.uk.

It can be difficult to find information about gallantry awards made to RFC, RNAS and RAF personnel. They are gazetted in the *London Gazette* (www.thegazette.co.uk), but citations are rarely given. There are, however, a few unindexed files containing citations which were presented to the

King for his formal approval in series AIR 2 (code 30). It might also be worth checking the squadron records in AIR 1. Details of awards to RNAS personnel are available in Ancestry's naval medals collection.

Operational Records

There are several series of operational records for the RFC, RNAS and RAF. Most records are to be found in series AIR 1 at Kew. Of particular importance are the daily communiqués, which are often referred to as the 'comic cuts' by aircrew. They summarise the events of the previous twenty-four hours, including details of dogfights with enemy aircraft. A typical entry is the one for 31 March 1917:

> A reconnaissance of the 1st Brigade observed fires in Lievin, Willerval and one mile east of Roclincourt. Considerable train movement was seen behind Queant and Baralle in the early morning. A large explosion was observed at Crosilles and fires were seen burning in Pronville, Queant and in other places.
>
> Artillery co-operation 28 targets were dealt with by aeroplane observation. Artillery of the First Army obtained four direct hits on hostile batteries. Three gun pits were destroyed and three explosions were caused. One of which was very large.
>
> Artillery of the Third Army obtained 13 direct hits on hostile batteries, and damaged gun emplacements. Seven direct hits were obtained on trenches.
>
> Hostile aircraft – Major A.J.L. Scott, Squadron Commander 60 Squadron destroyed a hostile machine south-east of Arras, Capt C.T. Black, 60 Squadron assisted Major Scott. A second hostile aeroplane was destroyed NE of Arras by Lt W.A. Bishop, 60 Squadron. A patrol of three Nieuports, 29 Squadron, drove down a hostile machine out of control in the vicinity of Gavrelle. Two other German machines were forced to land after having been engaged by Lts Binnie and W.E. Molesworth both of 60 Squadron. (TNA AIR 1/2116/204/57)

Abbreviated editions of the communiqués were published in three volumes by Christopher Cole and Chaz Bowyer in the early 1990s.

During 1917 Billy Bishop, the great Canadian air ace, was serving with 60 Squadron RFC based near Arras. It was here that he shot down many of the seventy-two enemy aircraft that he was credited with during the First World War.

The surviving records of RFC/RNAS/RAF squadrons are unfortunately very patchy. If you are lucky you will find a records book, which describes what the squadron did day by day. They are largely in series AIR 1 at TNA.

Also of interest are the combat reports compiled by pilots, although they should be treated with some caution, as pilots tended to claim planes which they had not shot down. This was inevitable in the heat of battle when several British aircraft might be engaged in a dogfight with a single enemy plane. They are arranged by squadron and can be found in AIR 1. However some combat reports are missing. A not untypical report was submitted by Captain C.T. Black of 60 Squadron on 31 March 1917:

A dogfight over the lines. Such incidents improved the morale of the troops in the front line, and were important to ensuring the command of the air.

While leading an OP [Observation Patrol] and escorting one of our machines piloted by Major A.R. Scott I saw an Albatross Scout over Hesinil. Major Scott dived on this machine and I followed. I saw Major Scott fire his gun and then bank away from the HA [hostile aircraft]. I followed the HA on his dive to the height of 1000 feet and fired a drum into him at 50 yards range. The last I saw of the HA he was diving vertically down to earth. I looked about for the rest of the patrol but could not find them, so I came back on this side of the line around Arras. I landed at Larbret short of petrol. (TNA AIR 1/225/204/5/2634)

In recent years there have been a number of squadron histories and websites, which are well worth checking out.

A major source for First World War military aviation is the RAF Museum. Of particular interest is their Story Vault website www.raf museumstoryvault.org.uk, which contains much about the war, including copies of casualty cards and the Air Force List for April 1918. More material will be added in due course. In addition the museum has many collections of private papers, photographs, books and other material,

A combat report prepared by Captain C T Black, 60 Squadron RFC, of a dog fight which took place on 31 March 1917. (*TNA AIR 1/1225/204/5/2634*)

although it has to be said that their Navigator catalogue is not easy to navigate.

Some material, particularly collections of aerial photographs, can be found at the Imperial War Museum. The IWM has some collections of papers for RAF personnel as well, such as those of the aviation and naval artist Harold Wylie, who kept an informative (but hard to read) diary. On 1 July 1916 he wrote:

> Went on reconnaissance 3.15pm to find out whether reinforcements were being sent up road. Ordered to stay over two hours. Unfortunately we had to carry four bombs which spoilt our climbing. Went over lines at 7500 [feet]. Dropped bombs as soon as possible and got to 8000. Shelled heavily going over…. As we were recrossing the line we saw that Gopsill was in great danger from an Albatross that was coming up behind him. We immediately dived 1000 feet at him and got off a burst. The others did the same and after another dive and burst the Hun made off for Plouvain. We were being very badly shelled at the time but managed to get back into some sort of formation and all got over the lines safely but low down.

Casualties

The Commonwealth War Graves Commission records the deaths of pilots and other air personnel. In particular the Flying Services Memorial in the Faubourg D'Arras Cemetery in northern France commemorates nearly 1,000 airmen who have no known grave.

The Air History website has a number of databases, including lists of RFC and RNAS fatalities, casualty reports and the casualty book maintained by RFC HQ in France. This records serious injuries to personnel incurred while flying, and missing aircrew. It was updated when further information came to light, such as a German report on the fate of missing aircrew.

Reports of aircraft (and pilot) casualties on the Western Front between March 1916 and April 1919 are in AIR 1/843-860, 865 with other lists in AIR 1/914-916, 960-969. The RAF Museum holds an extensive set of record cards relating to deaths, injuries and illness suffered by Royal

Flying Corps and Royal Air Force personnel, which are now online at www.rafmuseumstoryvault.org.uk.

Further Reading

Michael Foley, *Pioneers of Aerial Combat: Air Battles of the First World War* (Pen & Sword, 2013)
Norman Franks, *Great War Fighter Aces 1914–1916* (Pen & Sword, 2014)
Peter Hart, *Somme Success: The Royal Flying Corps and the Battle of the Somme 1916* (Pen & Sword, 2012)
Trevor Henshaw, *The Sky Their Battlefield* (2nd edition, 2014). More details at http://theskytheirbattlefield2.com.
Cecil Lewis, *Sagittarius Rising* (1936, republished Frontline Books, 2009)
Phil Tomaselli, *Tracing Your RAF Ancestors* (Pen & Sword, 2009)

Many invaluable resources about the RFC and RAF can be consulted on the Air History website at www.airhistory.org.uk/rfc/index.html. In addition www.theaerodrome.com and www.wwiaviation.com may also be able to help. Cross and Cockade is a society devoted to researching the war in the air. You can find out more at www.crossandcockade.com (the website also includes a number of useful resources).

Chapter 7

RESEARCHING DOMINION AND INDIAN TROOPS

The First World War involved participants from many different nations. In particular men, and a few women, from all four corners of the British Empire came to help the Mother Country.

When Britain declared war on 4 August 1914 she did so on behalf of the Empire as well as the United Kingdom itself. The five dominions – Australia, Canada, Newfoundland, New Zealand and South Africa – were self-governing, but left their defence and foreign affairs to the British Government. In part this reflected a belief among most Australians and Canadians that they were as British as any Londoner, Dubliner or Glaswegian. So it was natural that when the call came the dominions would not be found wanting, although recent studies have found that a high proportion of the Canadian and Australian troops, in particular, had been born in Britain and so presumably had closer ties to the home country than did men who were native to Canada or Australia. And occasionally you may find British men who managed to enlist in the colonial forces because the pay was better and the discipline less irksome. But wherever they came from, these 'colonial troops' were often regarded as the crack troops of the British Army.

The semi-autonomous Indian Empire, based in New Delhi, maintained the Indian Army under the direct control of the Viceroy. The Army was largely led by British officers, with native troops as ordinary soldiers and non-commissioned officers. Units from the Indian Army were rushed into the front line in the autumn and winter of 1914. By the spring of 1915 they had largely left France for the Middle East.

There were also small numbers of colonial troops in the front line, such as white Rhodesians and Fijian planters. West Indian and Chinese labourers were also recruited to work behind the lines, although very few records survive for these men.

In general the records are very similar to those you may be familiar with when researching British servicemen or British army units.

There are some shared records:

- The Commonwealth War Graves Commission record the last resting place of all Dominion and Indian troops;
- Gallantry awards for all ranks, and the commissions and promotion of officers in Dominion forces, appear in the *London Gazette*.
- Copies of war diaries of some Anzac units are at The National Archives in series WO 95, although the quality of the copying is poor.
- British newspapers often included stories about local men who had joined Dominion forces.

Australia

The National Archives of Australia hold service documents for, among other formations, the 1st Australian Imperial Force (AIF), Australian Flying Corps, Australian Army Nursing Service, and Depot or home records for personnel who served within Australia. The records are at www.naa.gov.au/collection/explore/defence/service-records/army-wwi. aspx. Also of interest is the AIF Project, which lists the details of those who served overseas with the Australian Imperial Force (www.aif.adfa. edu.au).

The Australian War Memorial (www.awm.gov.au) has a superb collection of material relating to Australian forces since 1901. Many records have been indexed or digitised, and placed online free of charge. You can find details at www.awm.gov.au/collection/digitised-record.

They include:

- A roll of honour with some personnel details
- First World War Embarkation Roll which contains details of approximately 330,000 AIF personnel as they left on overseas service
- First World War Nominal Roll with details of 324,000 AIF personnel who served overseas
- Honours and Awards with details of recommendations made to members of the AIF
- War diaries compiled by Australian units
- Official histories commissioned by the Australian government

The entrance and Commemorative Courtyard of the Australian War Memorial in Canberra. On panels in the arcade are the names of Australians who have died in wars since 1884. (*Author*)

Through the Anzac Collections programme the Memorial is digitising the personal papers and diaries of 150 Anzacs. Details are at www.awm. gov.au / 1914-1918 / anzac-connections.

Also available are the papers of General John Monash. By profession a civil engineer, he became one of the war's outstanding commanders. His papers give a comprehensive view of his wartime military career.

The National Library of Australia's Trove website (www.trove. nla.gov.au) is a brilliant resource with digitised newspapers, books, photographs and personal papers. As might be expected, there is a lot of material about the Australians on the Western Front, including newspaper reports, contemporary books and photographs.

There are also a number of excellent websites devoted to the Anzacs. Start with www.ww1westernfront.gov.au, which is an impressive well-written and well-researched site devoted to the Anzacs in Western Europe and the new Australian Remembrance Trail. The Australian War Memorial (www.awm.org.au) has masses of information about the Australian (and to an extent New Zealand) involvement in France, although it is not always easy to find.

Official histories prepared by both the Australian and New Zealand governments in the early 1920s can be downloaded from the Internet Archive free of charge.

Further Reading

Bill Gammage, *The Broken Years: Australian Soldiers in the Great War* (Penguin, 1975)

Neil Smith, *That Elusive Digger: tracing your Australian Military Ancestors* (Unlock the Past, 2013)

Canada

Library and Archives Canada holds many records for men and women who served in Canadian forces during the First World War. An increasing proportion are available through the Collections Canada portal (www.collectionscanada.ca). Unfortunately the databases are not always easy to use and the information available is partial. Before you start it might be worth looking at their First World War Search Topic, which explains what is available, at www.collectionscanada.gc.ca/genealogy/022-909.006-e.html.

Over 600,000 men and women enlisted in the Canadian Expeditionary Force (CEF) during the First World War (1914–1918) as soldiers, nurses and chaplains. At the time of writing Library and Archives Canada (LAC) is digitising all their service files. They expect to complete the work in the

A sculpture at the Canadian National Memorial at Vimy Ridge. The striking memorial commemorates the 60,000 who died in France and the 11,000 Canadians with no known grave. It was designed by Toronto architect W.S. Allward and unveiled by King Edward VIII in July 1936. (*Author*)

next few years. Unfortunately the records have been heavily weeded, and only key documents survive.

Also available are the war diaries for Canadian units, all of which have long been digitised. You can find them at www.collectionscanada.gc.ca/archivianet/02015202_e.html.

The Canadian Virtual War Memorial, www.vac-acc.gc.ca/remembers/sub.cfm?source=collections/virtualmem contains details of Canadians who died in the war and their last resting place. The information is similar to that available from the Commonwealth War Graves Commission. In addition the website also has pages about Canada during the First World War. Possibly of more use are the Circumstances of Death files for individuals, which are available at www.ancestry.ca (British subscribers will need to pay extra to use the databases), although unindexed records are available on the Collections Canada website.

The memorial to nearly 5,000 missing Indian troops at Neuve-Chapelle. It was designed by Sir Herbert Baker and unveiled in 1927. (*Tourisme Nord-Pas de Calais/R. Valmont*)

Further Reading

Glenn Wright, *Canadians at War 1914–1918: A Research Guide to War Service Records* (Global Genealogy Press, 2010)

New Zealand

Personnel records of 120,000 men who served in the New Zealand Expeditionary Force and were discharged before the end of 1920 are held by Archives New Zealand. They can be downloaded from http://archway.archives.govt.nz, alt. In addition the archives have nominal and casualty rolls, rolls of honour, a few unit (war) diaries (although most were destroyed in 1931) and records relating to honours and awards, which are briefly described in a research guide at http://archives.govt.nz/research/guides/war#first. Some regimental and official histories for New Zealand are available at http://nzetc.victoria.ac.nz/tm/scholarly/tei-corpus-WH1.html

New Zealand troops somewhere in France during the Hundred Days of the summer and autumn of 1918.

The UK National Archives has some war diaries for New Zealand units in series WO 95.

The Auckland War Memorial Museum's Cenotaph Database at http://muse.aucklandmuseum.com/databases/cenotaph has brief details about most New Zealand troops, particularly those who did not return. The database is being redeveloped for the centenary.

The National Library of New Zealand has digitised many of the country's newspapers, which are now available through the excellent Papers Past website (http://paperspast.natlib.govt.nz). The Library also has a very good introductory leaflet explaining how to research the war with links to key resources and archives (http://natlib.govt.nz/researchers/guides/first-world-war), as well as to those of the Library's own collections that have already been digitised. This includes several collections of photographs.

A useful general site on New Zealanders during the First World War is http://ww100.govt.nz/.

India

The location of the service records of Indian privates and non-commissioned officers is not known. A few Medal Index Cards survive, generally for men who served in colonial campaigns that took place in 1918 and 1919. These are available on both The National Archives website and Ancestry. The remainder of the cards are thought to have been destroyed.

Records for British officers in the Indian Army are at the British Library in London (www.bl.uk). In general there are many different sources for researching Indian soldiers, some of which duplicate information, and this can make research difficult.

Perhaps the best place to start is with an online database (http://indiafamily.bl.uk/UI) to British civil and military employees living in India, but it is by no means complete. Service records for officers and warrant officers are series IOL L/MIL/14. Some indexes are online at www.nationalarchives.gov.uk/a2a. However, it may be easier to use the British Library's catalogue to its own Archives and Manuscripts at http://searcharchives.bl.uk. War diaries for many Indian units who served in Flanders are in series WO 95 at Kew.

Further Reading

Emma Jolly, *Tracing Your British Indian Ancestors* (Pen & Sword, 2010)

Newfoundland

Library and Archives Canada holds many records for men and women who served in Canadian and Newfoundland forces during the First World War via the Collections Canada portal (www.collectionscanada.ca). Unfortunately the databases are not always easy to use and the information available is partial, but there is help at www.collections canada.gc.ca/genealogy/022-909.006-e.html.

Surviving service records of the Newfoundland Regiment are online at www.therooms.ca/regiment/part3_database.asp. War diaries are at The National Archives in Kew in piece WO 95/4312. There's a website devoted to the history of the regiment with more about the part it played on the Western Front, particularly at Beaumont-Hamel on 1 July 1916: www.rnfldr.ca/history.aspx?item=33.

South Africa

Service records are held by: South African National Defence Force, Documentation Service, Private Bag X289, Pretoria 0001, South Africa. Email sandfdoc@mweb.co.za.

There is very little online about men who served in the South African forces during the First World War. One exception is the excellent website of the South African Military History Society at http://samilitary history.org, which has much about the country's involvement in the First World War, including several articles about the battle of Delville Wood. It also provides details of the various military museums in South Africa.

On being wounded

Lt Liveing wrote of how he was cared for after being wounded on the battlefield. His sergeant had carried him back across No Man's Land.

The engine started, and we set off on our journey to the Casualty Clearing Station. For the last time we passed the villages, which we had come to know so intimately in the past two months during rest from the trenches. There was Souastre, where one had spent pleasant evenings at the Divisional Theatre; St Amand with its open square in front of the church, the meeting-place of the villagers, now deserted save for two or three soldiers; Gaudiempré, the headquarters of an Army Service Corps park, with its lines of roughly made stables. At one part of the journey a 15-inch gun let fly just over the road. We had endured quite enough noise for that day, and I was glad that it did not occur again. From a rather tortuous course through by-lanes we turned into the main Arras-to-Doullens road – that long, straight, typical French highway with its avenue of poplars. Shortly afterwards the ambulance drew up outside the Casualty Clearing Station.

The Casualty Clearing Station was situated in the grounds of a chateau. I believe that the chateau itself was used as a hospital for those cases which were too bad to be moved farther. We were taken into a long cement-floored building, and laid down in a line of stretchers which ran almost from the doorway up to a screen at the end of the room, behind which dressings and operations were taking place. On my right was the officer of the K__'s, still

---

fairly cheery, though in a certain amount of pain; on my left lay a rifleman hit in the chest, and very grey about the face; I remember that, as I looked at him, I compared the colour of his face with that of the stomach cases I had seen. A stomach case, as far as I can remember, has an ashen pallor about the face; a lung case has a haggard grey look. Next to him a boy of about eighteen was sitting on his stretcher; he was hit in the jaw, the arms, and the hands, but he calmly took out his pipe, placed it in his blood-stained mouth, and started smoking. I was talking to the officer of the K__'s, when he suddenly fell to groaning, and rolled over on to my stretcher. I tried to comfort him, but words were of no avail. A doctor came along, asked a few questions, and examined the wound, just a small hole in the pit of the stomach; but he looked serious enough about it. The stretcher was lifted up and its tortured occupant borne away behind the screen for an operation. That was the last I saw of a very plucky young fellow. I ate some bread and jam, and drank some tea doled out liberally all down the two lines of stretchers, for another line had formed by now.

My turn came at last, and I was carried off to a table behind the screen, where the wound was probed, dressed, and bandaged tightly, and I had a foretaste of the less pleasant side of hospital life. There were two Army nurses at work on a case next to mine – the first English women I had seen since I returned from leave six months before. My wound having been dressed, I was almost immediately taken out and put into a motor-lorry. There must have been about nine of us, three rows of three, on the floor of that lorry. I did not find it comfortable, though the best had been done under the circumstances to make it so; neither did the others, many of whom were worse wounded than myself, judging by the groans which arose at every jolt.

We turned down a road leading to the station. Groups of peasants were standing in the village street and crying after us: 'Ah! les pauvres blessés! Les pauvres Anglais blessés!' These were the last words of gratitude and sympathy that the kind peasants could give us. We drew up behind other cars alongside the hospital train, and the engine-driver looked round from polishing his engine and watched us with the wistful gaze of one to whom hospital train work was no longer a novelty. Walking wounded came dribbling up by ones and twos into the station yard, and were directed into sitting compartments.

The sun was in my eyes, and I felt as if my face was being scorched. I asked an RAMC NCO, standing at the end of the wagon, to get me something to shade my eyes. Then occurred what I felt was an extremely thoughtful act on the part of a wounded man. A badly wounded lance-corporal, on the other side of the lorry, took out his handkerchief and stretched it over to me. When I asked him if he was sure that he did not want it, he insisted on my taking it. It was dirty and blood-stained, but saved me much discomfort, and I thanked him profusely. After about ten minutes our stretchers were hauled out of the lorry. I was borne up to the officers' carriage at the far end of the train. It was a splendidly equipped compartment; and when I found myself between the sheets of my berth, with plenty of pillows under me, I felt as if I had definitely got a stage nearer to England. Some one behind me called my name, and, looking round, I saw my old friend M__ W__, whose party I had nearly run into the night before in that never-to-be-forgotten communication trench, Woman Street. He told me that he had been hit in the wrist and leg. Judging by his flushed appearance, he had something of a temperature.

More wounded were brought or helped in – men as well as officers – till the white walls of the carriage were lined with blood-stained, mud-covered khaki figures, lying, sitting, and propped up in various positions.

The Medical Officer in charge of the train came round and asked us what we should like to drink for dinner.

'Would you like whisky-and-soda, or beer, or lemonade?' he questioned me. This sounded pleasant to my ears, but I only asked for a lemonade.

As the train drew out of the station, one caught a last glimpse of warfare – an aeroplane, wheeling round in the evening sky amongst a swarm of tell-tale smoke-puffs, the explosions of 'Archie' shells.

Taken from Edward D. Liveing, *Attack! A Subaltern's Impressions of July 1, 1916* (New York, 1918)

Chapter 8

BATTLEFIELD TOURISM

If you can you really should get to the battlefields to see for yourself where the men fought. And once you go you will probably want to go again, because there is a unique appeal. As early as 1920, T.A. Lowe, who wrote one of the first guides to the Western Front, assured readers that:

> touring the battlefields is a different thing altogether to touring for the purpose of sight-seeing. In fact I can safe say that the mere sightseer will probably be disappointed with the devastated zones of France and Belgium. But combined with 'atmosphere' and imagination they will draw the tourists like magnets and [they] will probably return to them again and again.

All Commonwealth War Graves are well signposted. This sign is just outside the village of Fromelles. (*Author*)

Although the 'devastated areas' have long since been transformed into comfortable villages and slightly down-at-heel towns, the atmosphere remains. It only takes a little imagination to rekindle the events of a century ago. The highlights are undoubtedly the immaculately kept Commonwealth War Graves Cemeteries and the museums.

Apart from a few German fortifications that proved impossible to demolish, the occasional shell hole which has become a farm pond, and the very occasional strip of trench, notably at Beaumont-Hamel and Vimy Ridge, there are now very few reminders of the devastation that the war brought to the region. However, tons of shrapnel pieces, bullets and the occasional shell are still found each year by farmers. If you walk the fields you may see them for yourself. The French Army is still decommissioning hundreds of tonnes of munitions every year. If you are interested there is a display of recently recovered materiel at the Historal in Peronne.

A display at the Historal in Peronne of some of the munitions – the 'iron harvest' – that is still being recovered each year from the fields of the Somme.

German war cemeteries have a very different atmosphere to their British counterparts. This is the cemetery at Neuville-St Vaast near Arras. Jewish soldiers are remembered by a Star of David rather than a cross. (*Author*)

The Historal in Peronne is the best museum about the First World War in France. It is located in the town's castle, which is off the main square.

It is surprisingly easy to get to France from almost anywhere in Britain. During the war itself men going on leave were often home within twenty-four hours of leaving the trenches, despite the slowness of the trains back from the front. Today of course the journey takes a fraction of the time, using the Channel Tunnel or cross-Channel ferries. To do justice to the battlefields you really need a car, because public transport is sparse, although there are train stations in Lille, Amiens

A street sign in Peronne commemorating the liberation of the town by the Australians in October 1918.

and Arras, and a rudimentary bus service. The roads are fairly narrow, but many have recently been improved in anticipation of the centenary.

It is also possible to cycle or walk around the battlefields, which brings the visitor not only to the places where the armies clashed, but also to the landscape of monuments, cemeteries and villages that make the Somme battlefield, in particular, so moving to explore. If you are thinking of doing this, look out for Paul Reed's books *Walking Arras* (Pen & Sword, 2007) and *Walking the Somme* (2nd edition, Pen & Sword, 2011), as well as John Cooksey and Jerry Murland's *The Retreat from Mons* (Pen & Sword, 2014) and *The Battles of French Flanders* (Pen & Sword, 2015). In the mid-1990s Richard Holmes did a series of excellent television programmes based on walks around various battlefields. Those for Arras, the Somme and Mons are now on YouTube. He also wrote several books accompanying the series.

There are a reasonable number of hotels, and more have been built in recent years, but even when I went on a press trip in March 2014 all accommodation had already been fully booked for July 2016 and the tourist authorities were very worried about coping with the numbers of visitors they expected to turn up unannounced.

Since the 1970s a number of British couples and families, fascinated by the area's history, have emigrated to France, particularly to Picardy, to run guest houses or tours. One of the first was Avril Williams, who arrived with her two daughters in 1972. She still runs a well-regarded bed and breakfast and tearooms in the small Somme village of Auchonvillers (www.avrilwilliams.eu). To an extent tourism to the Somme battlefields remains in British and Commonwealth hands. And it is safe to say that French officials have only recently come to realise the importance of battlefield tourism.

In any case, perhaps, it might be best to travel out of season, in part because it will be quieter, but also because, on a chilly windswept day with the threat of rain, you can get a real sense of what it must have been like a hundred years ago.

Both the Nord-Pas-de-Calais and Somme (Picardy) tourist boards have excellent websites with plenty of information about visiting the battlefields and links to hotels and attractions. As well as the battlefields this is an attractive part of France, often overlooked by British tourists, and there is lots to do and see. Try:

www.northernfrance-tourism.com
www.visit-somme.com
www.somme-battlefields.com

It is easy enough to organise a self-guided tour. The cemeteries in particular are well signposted. Or you can download an audioguide from Somme Tourism's website for two suggested routes around the key sites, or pick up a pre-loaded mp3 player from one of their offices. And in Nord-Pas-de-Calais there is a special website devoted to four Trails of Remembrance www.remembrancetrails-northernfrance.com. Details of a number of guidebooks are given below.

An alternative is to go on a guided tour, particularly if you are short of time. There are a number of tour companies that will pick you up at your hotel and take you to see the main sites or, if you ask, design a day or half-day tour to meet your specifications. Two of the best, according to TripAdvisor, are Terres de Memoire (www.terresdememoire.com) and Battlefields Experience (thebattleofthesomme.co.uk), both of which start in Amiens. Slightly further north in Arras there is Sacred Ground Tours (www.sacredgroundtours.com.au), but of course there are other companies who offer similar services.

Another popular way of travelling to the French battlefields is on a guided tour, which includes travel from the UK, hotels, meals and a guide. There are many companies that provide tours. Most offer general introductory tours, but it is possible to go on more specific trips, perhaps to study a particular battle or the war poets. The Western Front Association organises several tours each year. Details at www.westernfrontassociation.com/wfa-tours.html.

Here are five companies that regularly run tours, but no doubt there are others equally as good:

Battlefield Breaks – http://battlefield-breaks.com
Battle Honours – www.battle-honours.eu
Holts Tours – http://holts.co.uk
Leger Holidays – www.visitbattlefields.co.uk
Spirit of Remembrance – www.spiritofremembrance.com

If you have the money you can commission a bespoke tour, perhaps to visit the places an ancestor served or to look at a specific action in great detail. Matt Limb Battlefield Tours (www.mlbft.co.uk) is one company that can offer this service, which has been recommended. But again there are lots of alternatives.

To get full value you need to be sure that a member of the Guild of Battlefield Guides is leading the tour, as Guild members are extremely knowledgeable about the fighting and the area you are touring and are used to dealing with groups.

There is a surprising amount to do and see while you are there. I have included below a list of key sites with a couple of unusual choices. Unless indicated they lie on the Somme. The list is largely based on visits I have made to the battlefields over the years. I have given addresses, opening times and so on, but it is wise to check before you go.

There are several hundred Commonwealth War Graves Cemeteries, from tiny ones in churchyards to large cemeteries where thousands of men lie. Details of all British and Commonwealth war graves are available through the Commonwealth War Graves Commission website www.cwgc.org.

There are also countless memorials to units and individuals, which are just too many to list here. As far as I know there is no comprehensive list of memorials online, but most will be described in the Holts' guide.

One word of warning. You may well come across bullets, shrapnel and other munitions lying in fields on your visit. Do not pick them up as they can be dangerous. A friend of mine came down with mustard gas poisoning as a result of touching a shell. I kid you not. Every year or so there are stories about people being killed as shells or grenades explode when they move them. And as I was writing this chapter Eurostar services had been disrupted on two separate occasions because passengers had tried to bring shells from the battlefields in their backpacks through security at Lille and Paris Gare du Nord, causing the evacuation of the stations. You may be able to buy cleaned and safe souvenirs from museums and shops.

Must-see Places

Museums

Historal de la Grande Guerre
Château de Péronne
BP 20063
80201 PERONNE
http://en.historial.org
Open daily, except Wednesdays in winter
Admission charge

This superb museum tells the story of the First World War through the eyes of British, French and German soldiers over the four years of the war, although curiously there's little specifically about the battles on the Somme, as the emphasis is firmly on the social rather than the strategic side of the war. The museum has recently been redesigned and there is a lot of new material to see, as well as one or two temporary exhibitions each year.

Wellington Quarry/Carrière Wellington
Rue Arthur Deletoille
62000 Arras
No website, but details at www.greatwar.co.uk/french-flanders-artois/museum-wellington-quarry.htm
Open daily, except January. Admission charge

Prior to the Battle of Arras in the spring of 1917, British engineers carved out a maze of tunnels through the chalk under the German front lines on the edge of Arras. In it troops would wait until told to go over the top on 9 April 1917, with the intention of catching the enemy by surprise. Forgotten for decades, the tunnels were rediscovered and turned into this stunning and memorable museum. It's quite different to any other attraction on the Western Front. Groups are taken on hour-long tours through the maze of tunnels, stopping at various points of interest.

Also try the Arras and Flying Services memorials in the in the Faubourg d'Amiens British military cemetery, Boulevard de General de Gaulle. The Arras memorial commemorates 35,000 servicemen from the United

Kingdom, South Africa and New Zealand who have no known grave. Most were killed during the Allied offensive during the Battles of Arras in April and May 1917 and during the German attack the following March. The Flying Services memorial commemorates the 990 pilots and observers of the RFC, RNAS and RAF whose bodies were never found.

Sights

Beaumont-Hamel Newfoundland Memorial
Rue de l'Église (route D73)
80300 Beaumont-Hamel
Open daily
Free
http://tinyurl.com/m6z8t4n

Located just outside the village, this is one of the most visited sites on the Somme and for good reason. It commemorates the tragic sacrifice of the men of the Royal Newfoundland Regiment on 1 July 1916. The memorial takes the form of a giant elk. The memorial grounds also include the largest remaining segment of a trench system to be found anywhere on the Western Front. Even though decades of erosion have taken their toll, you can still see the trenches and shell holes. The field slopes down to a stream where, on the other side, the Germans were waiting. There is a visitors' centre and guided tours are available from friendly Canadian students.

Also try the Ocean Villas museum in the neighbouring village of Auchonvillers (10, Rue Delattre), which contains exhibits about the Somme in both world wars as well as a short example of a communication trench (www.avrilwilliams.eu). The museum is open daily and is next to Avril Williams' guesthouse and tearooms.

Thiepval Memorial
80300 Thiepval
www.historial.org
Open daily
Free

Theipval commemorates the men who fell on the Somme between July 1915 and March 1918 and who have no known grave. Some 72,205 British and South African names are to be found etched on Portland stone on the massive arches. The memorial was designed by the pre-eminent British architect of the day, Sir Edwin Lutyens. Many critics have argued that it is one of his finest works, although personally I find it a bit grandiose and cold. Attached is an excellent visitors' centre, which combines exhibitions about the battles and the Missing of the Somme database, as well as a shop and toilets.

Further reading: Gavin Stamp, *The Memorial to the Missing of the Somme* (Profile, 2006)

Also try the Ulster Memorial (see below) which is a short drive away.

Canadian National War Memorial
Vimy
Route D55
Open daily
Free

This gigantic and very impressive Art Deco memorial to 66,000 Canadians who made the ultimate sacrifice, with two massive columns and fine views over the French countryside, was dedicated by King Edward VIII in July 1936. It was built on Hill 145, which was captured by Canadian infantry after a bitter fight in April 1917.

The memorial is part of the 240-acre (116-hectare) Canadian Memorial Park which, as a whole, is also a must-visit destination. Here you will find a visitors' centre where you can walk through some excavated trenches to get a real sense of how claustrophobic and close to the German lines they were. Meanwhile sheep happily graze in parts of the park where the public are not allowed because there are still unexploded shells.

Visit if you can

Museums

Musée de la Bataille de Fromelles
Rue de la Basse Ville
59249 Fromelles
www.musee-bataille-fromelles.fr
Open daily, except Tuesdays
Admission charge

Adjacent to the Pheasant Wood Cemetery, this brand-new museum with some fascinating displays is devoted to the battle of Fromelles on 19 and 20 July 1916. In a few hours 5,500 Australian and 1,500 British soldiers were killed in one of the worst-planned attacks of the war. In 2009 250 bodies of some of the men who were killed were found in a local wood. They were subsequently buried in Pheasant Wood Cemetery, the first new CWGC cemetery on the Western Front for eighty years.

Also try the VC Corner Australian Cemetery and the Australian Memorial Park, in the same village.

Somme Trench Museum/Musée Somme 1916
Rue Anicet Godin
80300 Albert
www.musee-somme-1916.eu
Daily, except January
Admission charge

A surprisingly effective, although rather amateurish, museum showing life in the trenches. It is based in tunnels under the town of Albert, which provides a unique atmosphere.

Sites

Australian War Memorial
80800 Villiers-Bretonneaux
Open daily
Free

Designed by Sir Edwin Lutyens and unveiled in 1938 by George VI, this imposing white stone monument, with a Commonwealth Cemetery in the foreground, consists of a tall central tower with two corner pavilions linked to the tower by plain walls that bear the names of 11,000 Australian soldiers who fell in France, and whose graves are not known.

Also try the small but interesting Musée Franco-Australien in the village (9 rue de Victoria, www.museeaustralien.com). It is in the village school, which was rebuilt in the 1920s with contributions from the children of Victoria.

Delville Wood
5 route de Ginchy
80390 Longueval
www.delvillewood.com
Site open daily, although the museum and visitor's centre is closed on Mondays and in December and January

One of the bloodiest battles of the Somme Campaign took place in Delville Wood. The South Africans played a key role in capturing the wood, so it was natural that after the war the area would become their national memorial. A handsome museum opened in 1986. Look out for the hornbeam, the only tree to survive the battle. There is a small visitors' centre and café.

Lochnagar Crater
Route de la Grande Mine
80300 Orvillers-la-Boisselle
www.lochnagarcrater.org
Open daily
Free

This is an impressively large hole in the ground, set in a field by the edge of a road near the village. It is the result of a very large explosion that took place at 7.28am on 1 July 1916, obliterating 300 metres of German trenches. 60,000lbs (27,000kg) of explosives were used to make the largest crater ever created by man in anger.

Loos Memorial to the Missing
Dud Corner Cemetery
Route de Béthune
62528 Loos-en-Gohelle
Open daily
Free
www.greatwar.co.uk/french-flanders-artois/memorial-loos-memorial.htm

The Loos Memorial forms the side and back of Dud Corner Cemetery and commemorates over 20,000 officers and men who have no known grave, who fell in the area from the River Lys to the old southern boundary of the First Army, east and west of Grenay. The vast majority fell during the Battle of Loos, which took place during the autumn of 1915.

Interesting Places

Museums

Fort de Seclin
Chemin de Petit Fort
59113 Seclin
www.fortseclin.com
Open Sundays at 3pm between April and November. Otherwise by appointment.
Admission charge

This 1870s fort just to the south of Lille was occupied by Bavarian units until it was captured by the British in the dying days of the war. There's a small collection of artillery, but mostly it has a unique atmosphere, as if the Germans had just left.

Sites

Caverne du Dragon
D18 Chemin des Dames
02160 Oulches-La-Valleé-Foulon
www.caverne-du-dragon.fr
Open daily, except January
Admission charge

For three years German and French troops fought bitter battles in this former underground quarry under the Chemin des Dames battlefield. Even though no British troops were stationed here this is a memorable, and frankly still rather scary, place to visit.

German War Cemeteries
There are German cemeteries at Fricourt and Neuville St Vaast.
Open daily
Free

There are several sombre cemeteries which are memorials to the huge German losses suffered on the Western Front. The largest of these lies just north of the village of Fricourt. Men are buried in mass graves under black crosses (and the occasional Star of David). It is said the CWGC tried to recreate an English country garden in many of the cemeteries, while the Germans sought to create the feel of woodland glades. They are maintained by the Volksbund Deutsche Kriegsgräberfürsorge (www.volksbund.de). An interesting article about the Volksbund is at www.greatwar.co.uk/organizations/volksbund-vdk.htm.

Nécropole de Notre-Dame-De-Lorette
62153 Ablain-Saint-Nazaire (north of Arras)
Open daily
Free

This is the largest French cemetery on the Western Front, with 20,000 individual graves and the bones of 23,000 other men buried in eight ossuaries. It has a very different feel to any British war cemetery. A new interpretation centre, mainly about the battle of Artois, which chiefly involved the French and Germans in 1915, has opened in the village of Souchez, which you pass through as you drive up to the cemetery.

Ulster Memorial Tower
Route de Saint-Pierre-Divion
80300 Thiepval
www.belfastsomme.com
Open daily, except Monday. There is also a small café (recommended) and information centre
Free

The memorial to the men of the 36th (Ulster) Division is based on Helen's Tower, a well-known Northern Irish landmark at Clandeboye, Co. Down. New recruits drilled in the shadows of the Tower in the autumn of 1914. Behind the tower are the remains of some trenches.

Further Reading

If you are planning a trip you should visit the World War One Battlefields website, which has lots of background information, including an excellent short video on some of the key highlights (www.ww1battlefields. co.uk/somme.html) and various essays on Tom Morgan's Hellfire Corner (www.hellfirecorner.co.uk), recounting individual experiences of visiting the battlefields (and much more besides). Of particular interest are pieces by Charles Fair on some of the more unusual sites on the Marne and Aisne. Detailed and well-presented descriptions of almost all the sites, museums and related attractions can be found on the Great War website www.greatwar.co.uk. Paul Read has also put a guide to walking the Armentières to La Brasse sector at http://battlefields1418.50megs.com and there are also pages about other parts of the front in France.

There are a number of guidebooks available to help you find your way around. For the Western Front as a whole Rose Coombe's *Before Endeavours Fade* (After the Battle, 2006) is highly recommended for the breadth of its coverage. A more basic introduction, but still pretty comprehensive, is Bradt's *World War I Battlefields: A Travel Guide to the Western Front* (Bradt, 2014).

For the Somme itself the best guidebook is probably *Major and Mrs Holt's Battlefield Guide to the Somme* (Pen & Sword, 2008). Another in-depth guide is *The Middlebrook Guide to the Somme Battlefields: A Comprehensive Coverage from Crecy to the World Wars* (Pen & Sword, 2007). No doubt new editions will be available in time for the centenary in 2016. If you are going to the Marne, then you will need Andrew Uffindell, *The Marne: a Battlefield Guide* (Pen & Sword, 2013).

Maps

France is well mapped and there is a choice of maps covering the battlefield areas. Road atlases of France are readily available, but these may be too small-scale for a detailed tour. Michelin and IGN do a range of larger-scale maps for motorists. Of the two I prefer the IGN Series Vert (1:100,000 scale). If you are intending to walk or cycle IGN also publish Serie Bleue maps, which are large-scale (1:25,000) maps designed for walking and cycling tours. Sheets 2408 O, 2408 E and 2407 E, for example, cover the majority of the Somme battlefields. IGN also publish a small-scale thematic map showing the northern portion of the Western Front: 'Great War 1914–1918', which is useful for planning but is little real use on the ground. All these maps can be bought online from Maps of the World (www.mapsworldwide.com) or Stanfords map shop in London. Particularly if you are walking and cycling you should take a trench map or two to help orientate yourself in the landscape. G.H. Smith (www.ghsmithbookshop.com) has republished many maps.

Appendix 1

RESEARCHING WAR MEMORIALS

After the war some tens of thousands of war memorials were erected in honour of men who did not return. They are still common features in towns and villages. As well as those commemorating the dead from a particular town or area, there are many memorials for schools, churches or work places. They take many forms, not just the memorials commonly found in parks and churches, but also include hospitals, sports grounds and even woods.

An individual may appear on several memorials. Normally all you will find is his surname and Christian name or initials, but sometimes the rank and unit and details of gallantry medals will also be included. There's no national list of who appears where, although there were plans a few years ago to create such a list.

Although it is cunningly hidden on their website, the Imperial War Museum has a database of some 66,000 memorials at www.iwm.org.uk/memorials/search?query=war%20memorials. Individual entries can include a full transcript of the dedication and a physical description of the memorial and an account of why and how it came to be created. Sometimes there is a photograph as well. An increasing number of entries include listings of all the individuals to be found commemorated on the memorial.

There are about a thousand memorials that specifically mention the great battles in France, ranging from a plaque in the Albion Pub in Chester 'In Grateful Memory Of Thomas Hopley Killed In Action – Arras. March 1918 'Faithful Unto Death'' to a processional cross in St Cuthbert's Church, Fir Vale, Sheffield made from parts collected from the Somme battlefield after the battle. It was presented by Lt S.W. Maunder of the 12th York and Lancaster Regiment (Sheffield City Battalion) as a souvenir of the Somme battlefield.

Information about many war memorials, including images and brief histories, can also be found on the War Memorials Online website (www.warmemorialsonline.org.uk). You can upload images and details of war memorials in your area if they aren't already there. It is supported by the War Memorials Trust (www.warmemorialsonline.org.uk), which does much good work in conserving and protecting memorials.

If you are researching an Irish soldier then check out the Irish War Memorials website (www.irishwarmemorials.ie), which lists many memorials to the fallen, both North and South, and there are indexes to individuals and places.

Scotland's war dead are honoured at the Scots National War Memorial at Edinburgh Castle. More information can be found at www.snwm.org.

There are a number of websites and books devoted to the men who appear on specific war memorials. Two of the best websites I have come across are for memorials in Cheltenham (www.remembering.org.uk) and Wolverhampton (www.wolverhamptonwarmemorials.org.uk).

It is now quite common for local history groups or individuals to research the men who appear on war memorials. As I know from studying the war memorials of Kew this can be very rewarding, but it also presents a number of problems. The chief of these is working out why individuals appear on the memorials in the first place. You will often find men who seem to have no connection with the area, others who didn't die on active service, or, conversely, men who should appear but have been missed off. After nearly a century, unless the original paperwork survives (which is rare), the selection process remains a mystery. Lastly, you may find a man whom it is impossible to identify from Commonwealth War Graves Commission records.

A most unusual memorial to a dog. Foch was found wandering in trenches on the Somme and died a decade later in Richmond. (*Author*)

Also, it is inevitable that in many cases you won't find very much about the lives, service and circumstances of the death of many of those on the memorial.

Records you will need to use to research war memorials:

- Commonwealth War Graves Commission website
- Local newspapers
- Local records (where they survive) such as memorial committee minutes, council minutes and the like
- Service records
- War diaries (and equivalents)
- 1911 Census for family details

Soldiers Died In The Great War

Records relating to individual casualties listed in Soldiers Died are available on Ancestry and Findmypast (see Chapter 3). However, it is perfectly possible to manipulate the database to produce lists of men from particular units or towns. To do this you need to obtain a copy of Soldiers Died on CD from Military and Naval Press (for more details see www.great-war-casualties.com). Alternatively, some local libraries, family history society research centres and Western Front Association branches may also have copies.

Appendix 2

THE MEN

The stories of the following men, as found in the records, are woven throughout the book to illustrate the sort of material that can be turned up about individuals. What links them is that they have left something tangible behind: memoirs, papers or, as in the case of John Mayberry, just his name absent-mindedly carved into the church wall at Soupir on the Aisne, perhaps during a lull in the fighting on 14–15 September 1914.

A bored Private John Mayberry, Connaught Rangers, etched his name with a penknife in the church wall at Soupir while awaiting a German attack in September 1914. (*Author*)

Captain William Henry Johnston VC, Royal Engineers

Lieutenant Edward G D Liveing, 12th London Regiment

R/9885 Rifleman Giles Eyre, 2nd King's Royal Rifle Corps

3991 Pte Alfred Dyson Freeman, Honourable Artillery Company

241076 Pte Thomas Hopley, Cheshire Regiment

9003 Pte John Mayberry, 2nd Connaught Rangers

5225 Sgt John William Streets, 12th York and Lancaster Regiment (Sheffield City Battalion)

5357 L/Cpl Joseph John Streets, 1/14th London Regiment (London Scottish)

10799 Pte Theodore Veale VC, 8th Devonshire Regiment

Appendix 3

THE TIMELINE

Given below are details of the major battles that took place along the Western Front in France. More information about these battles can be found on Wikipedia or in the books recommended in the bibliography. Even in quiet sectors there were also regular trench raids and skirmishes in no man's land, details of which can be found in the unit war diaries.

Name of battle	Dates	Notes	Number of British casualties
Marne	5–12 September 1914	The battle effectively brought the German advance towards Paris to an end. It led to the 'Race to the Sea' and the creation of the defensive trench systems which became the Western Front.	80,000
Neuve Chapelle	10–13 March 1915	This was the first British-led offensive of the war. Initial progress was rapid, but the advance was reversed because the success could not be exploited.	11,000 British and Indian
Loos	25 September–14 October 1915	At the time this was the biggest battle in the British Army's history. The first British use of poison gas occurred and the battle was the first mass engagement of New Army units. The British offensive was part of the attempt by the French to break through the German defences and restore a war of movement. However, the Franco-British attacks were contained by the Germans.	72,000
Somme	1 July–18 November 1916	One of the bloodiest battles in history, the British and French objectives were to seize German defences above the Somme river and, frankly, to kill more Germans than they killed Tommies and Poilu. On the opening day the British Army suffered the worst losses in its history.	419,654

Name of battle	Dates	Notes	Number of British casualties
Ancre	13–18 November 1916	The last and successful gasp of the Battle of the Somme in which Anglo-French forces used new tactics to press their advantage with several smaller attacks in quick succession, rather than pausing to regroup and thus giving the German armies time to recover.	Roughly 20,000
Arras	9 April–16 May 1917	On Easter Sunday British and Dominion troops attacked German defences near Arras. There were major gains in the first few days, followed by stalemate. This is reckoned to be a British victory, but it had very little impact on the strategic or tactical situation on the Western Front.	158,660
Cambrai	20 November–8 December 1917	Cambrai saw the first effective use of tanks by the British. Three hundred tanks were in action on the first day. As so often the British made significant gains on the first day, but were unable to capitalise on their achievements. By the end of the battle the Germans had recaptured most of their early losses.	47,596

German Spring Offensive	21 March–12 June 1918	On 21 March the Germans launched a massive attack along the Western Front, which marked the deepest advances by either side since 1914. The main thrust was through the British lines towards Amiens. Ultimately the Offensive failed because the Germans did not have the reserves to consolidate their advances. The Allies were hurt, but unbeaten.	539,739 (British, French and American casualties)
Amiens	8–12 August 1918	Amiens was the opening phase of the Hundred Days Offensive that ultimately led to victory. Allied forces advanced over seven miles on the first day, one of the greatest advances of the war. This led Erich Ludendorff to describe the first day of the battle as 'the black day of the German Army'. Amiens was one of the first major battles involving armoured warfare and marked the end of trench warfare on the Western Front.	22,000 (British, French and American casualties)

Sources: Wikipedia. Scott Addington, *The Great War 100: the First World War in Infographics* (The History Press, 2014)

BIBLIOGRAPHY

Books

There must be several thousand books about the Western Front, and in particular the Battle of the Somme, and the men who fought there. The first came out within months of the outbreak of war. And no doubt many more will be published to coincide with the centenary. As well as editions in hardback or paperback most of the titles described below are also available as e-books, ideal for you to take with you to the battlefields.

Pen & Sword, the publishers of this book, have a number of books on the battles in France. You may find them in museum bookshops and at the excellent bookshop at The National Archives, but in general it is best to order them online at www.pen-and-sword.co.uk. And of course your local bookshop should be able to obtain them for you.

Out-of-print books can be sourced through Abebooks (www.abebooks.co.uk), which has access to the catalogues of hundreds of booksellers worldwide.

The Battle of the Somme

Geoff Dyer, *The Missing of the Somme* (Phoenix, 2001)

Peter Barton, *The Somme: The Untold Story in Never Before Seen Panoramas* (Constable, 2011)

Joshua Levine, *Forgotten Voices of the Somme: The Most Devastating Battle of the Great War in the Words of Those Who Survived* (Ebury, 2008)

Peter Hart, *Somme Success: The Royal Flying Corps and the Battle of the Somme 1916* (Pen & Sword, 2013)

Peter Hart and Nigel Steel, *The Somme* (Cassell, 2012)

Lyn Macdonald, *Somme* (Penguin, 1993)

Martin Middlebrook, *The First Day on the Somme* (Allen Lane, 1971)

William Philpott, *Bloody Victory: The Sacrifice on the Somme and the Making of the Twentieth Century* (Abacus, 2010)

Andrew Rawson, *The Somme Campaign* (Pen & Sword, 2014)

Andrew Robertshaw, *Somme 1 July 1916: Tragedy and Triumph* (Osprey, 2008)

Joe Sacco, *The Great War July 1, 1916: The First Day Of The Battle Of The Somme An Illustrated Panorama* (Jonathan Cape, 2013)

Jack Sheldon, *The German Army on the Somme 1914–1916* (Pen & Sword, 2007)

Gary Sheffield, *The Somme* (Cassell, 2003)

If I had to choose just one title I'd go for Andrew Robertshaw.

Other Battles and Campaigns

Pierre Berton, *Vimy* (Pen & Sword, 2012)

Geoff Bridger, *Neuve Chapelle* (Pen & Sword, 1998)

Peter Doyle, *Loos 1915* (The History Press, 2012)

Bryn Hammond, *Cambrai 1917* (Weidenfeld & Nicolson, 2009)

Peter Hart, *1918: A Very British Victory* (Weidenfeld & Nicolson, 2008)

Chris McNab, *Battle Story Cambrai 1917* (The History Press, 2012)

Martin Middlebrook, *The Kaiser's Battle: 21 March 1918: The First Day of the German Spring Offensive* (Penguin, 1983)

Jonathan Nichols, *Cheerful Sacrifice: the Battle of Arras 1917* (Pen & Sword, 2005)

Barrie Pitt, *1918: the last act* (Pen & Sword, 2014)

Philip Warner, *The Battle of Loos* (Pen & Sword, 2009)

Tourist Guides

Major and Mrs Holt's Pocket Battlefield Guide to the Somme 1916/1918 (Pen & Sword, 2008)

John Ruler, *World War I Battlefields: A Travel Guide to the Western Front: Sites, Museums, Memorials* (Bradt, 2014)

Paul Reed, *Walking the Somme* (Pen & Sword, 2011)

Thomas Scotland and Steven Hays, *Understanding the Somme: an Illuminating Battlefield Guide* (Hellion, 2014)

The British Army

Richard Holmes, *Tommy: the British Soldier on the Western Front* (Harper, 2011)

Andrew Rawson, *The British Army 1914–1918* (The History Press, 2014)

Andrew Robertshaw, *24 Hour Trench: A Day in the Life of Tommy* (The History Press, 2012)

Memoirs and Diaries (a small selection of books currently in print)

Giles Eyre, *Somme Harvest: Memories of a P.B.I. in the Summer of 1916* (1938, reprinted Naval and Military Press, 2001)

E.P.F. Lynch, *Somme Mud* (Transworld, 2010)

Max Plowman, *A Subaltern on the Somme* (Naval and Military Press, 2001)

Sidney Rogerson, *Twelve Days on the Somme: A Memoir of the Trenches, 1916* (1933, reprinted Greenhill, 2006)

John F. Tucker, *Johnny Get Your Gun: A Personal Narrative of the Somme, Ypres and Arras* (1978, reprinted Pen & Sword, 2015)

General Histories of the First World War

There are numerous general histories of the war that are worth looking at if you want to put the Somme into context.

Scott Addington, *The Great War 100: the First World War in Infographics* (The History Press, 2014)

Arthur Banks, *A Military Atlas of the First World War* (1975, reprinted Pen & Sword, 2014)

Ian Connarty et al, *At The Going Down of the Sun* (Lannoo, 2001)

Peter Hart, *The Great War 1914–18* (Profile, 2014)

Richard Holmes, *The Western Front* (BBC, 2008)

Ian Palmer, *The Salient: Ypres 1914–1918* (Constable, 2007)

David Reynolds, *The Long Shadow: The Legacies of the Great War in the Twentieth Century* (Norton, 2014)

Gary Sheffield, *Forgotten Victory: The First World War: Myths and Realities* (Headline, 2001)

David Stevenson, *1914–1918: The History of the First World War* (Penguin, 2012)

Hew Strachan, *The First World War* (Simon & Schuster, 2014)

Tim Travers, *The Killing Ground* (Pen & Sword, 2009)

Websites

There are a number of websites that can help your research, most of which are listed in the appropriate place in the book . However, Wikipedia has some excellent pages on the Western Front and the battles that were fought there. For all aspects of the British Army and its organisation you need to use Chris Baker's superb Long Long Trail site (www.1914-1918.net). Paul Nixon's Army Ancestry Research blog at http://army ancestry.blogspot.co.uk has a lot about the minutiae of Army records.

The Western Front Association's website (www.westernfrontassociation. com) has masses of information about all aspects of the war and they welcome contributions from members and non-members alike.

Also of interest are the Great War (www.greatwar.co.uk) and Hellfire Corner (www.hellfirecorner.co.uk) websites, although here the emphasis is more on the battles and battlefield tourism. Writer Paul Read's website The Old Front Line also has some interesting pages (http://battlefields 1418.50megs.com).

The WW1 Photos website www.ww1photos.com contains many photos of individual officers and soldiers, with the occasional transcript from books and indexes. Extracts from a number of personal diaries of the period are at www.war-diary.com and documents and images relating to the Somme are at http://leoklein.com/itp/somme/

The Western Front Association

If you become passionate about the First World War you should consider joining the Western Front Association. The Association exists to further interest in the First World War and aims to perpetuate the memory, courage and comradeship of all those on all sides who served their countries in France and Flanders. Members are a mixture of academics, enthusiasts and family historians. The Association publishes four journals and four comprehensive newsletters a year, runs several conferences and now maintains an excellent and informative website at www.western frontassociation.com. At time of writing membership is £26 per annum.

INDEX